Shania Twain

S

Shania Twain

MICHAEL McCALL
photo research by Raeanne Rubenstein

St Martin's Griffin ⚜ *New York*

Design by Bonni Leon-Berman

ISBN 0-312-20673-9

First St. Martin's Griffin Edition: June 1999

10 9 8 7 6 5 4 3 2 1

TO MARY JEAN,
for everything you've given me

Contents

Acknowledgments *ix*

Chapter One
For the First Time *1*

Chapter Two
From a Faraway Place *17*

Chapter Three
On My Way *35*

Chapter Four
Mercury Rising *45*

Chapter Five
The Woman in Her *65*

Chapter Six
Come One, Come All *123*

Chapter Seven
A Diva, After All *149*

Acknowledgments

The author wishes to thank Dana Albarella, Madeleine Morel, Raeanne Rubenstein, Mary Bailey, Barbara Carr, Jon Landau, Luke Lewis, Sandy Neese, Lisa Wannish, Kevin Lane, Chris Stacey, John Grady, Ron Baird, Dick Frank, Norro Wilson, David Hartt, Maureen Yakabuski, Olaf Karl, Frances Preston, Roger Sovine, Ellen Wood, Jim Ed Norman, Mike Curb, Stuart Colman, Donna Tauscher, Jonathan Marx, Jim Ridley, Bill Friskics-Warren, Lyndsey Parker, *McLean's* magazine, Jay Orr, Rboert K. Oermann, Tom Roland, Bruce Feiler, James Hunter, Jack Hurst, Dave Hoekstra, Chet Flippo, Lon Helton, and Calvin Gilbert.

I also want to express endless gratitude to my family: Mary Jean, Douglas and Anna; Charles and Helen McCall; Michelle and Brian Olton; Craig and Renee

Acknowledgments

McCall and my nieces Alison, Kaylee, and Samantha; Monica and Erin Monet; Mark McCall; Randy McCall; Linda Gail Lewis; Eddie Braddock; Annie and Oliver Dolan; Cecil Harrelson; Lois Harrelson; Edna Festervand; Cecil Harrelson Jr.; and Lois, Rebecca, and Jamie Skains.

Shania Twain

Chapter One

For the First Time

AFTER ALL THIS TIME, AFTER ALL THE RUMORS and promises, Shania Twain wanted to make her arrival count. She wanted her entry onto the stage for her long-awaited concert debut as a superstar to carry as much attitude as her songs.

So here she came, sitting royally on an ornate chair with four muscle-bound men carrying her aloft on a platform, rushing through the aisles and delivering her to the stage, where her shining kingdom awaited. As she leapt from the chair and bounded across the Sudbury Community Arena stage, through the flashing multicolored lights, her adoring flock wildly roared its approval. Calls of "We love you, Shania," rang out and bodies surged forward.

Shania purposely chose to introduce her first international concert extravaganza in Sudbury, Ontario, a small Northern Ontario mining town 180 miles south of her hometown, Timmins. Sudbury was where a young Shania—then known as Eilleen Twain to her friends and family—would drive with friends to see concerts in her youth, big-ticket, big-concept shows by such theatrical rock 'n' roll acts as Pink Floyd, Rush, and Jethro Tull.

Today, in Northern Ontario, Shania is considered royalty. Sudbury declared May 29, 1998, as Shania Twain day, and townsfolk considered her premiere concert the most glamorous event ever to hit the hard-drinking, blue-collar town of 93,000.

How big of a deal was it? The local newspaper, *The Sudbury Star*, called Shania's show "the biggest thing to hit this town since they dug the Creighton mine," a reference to the local nickel mine and the economic center of the area.

Jim Hamm, program director of country station CIGM-AM, said, "For a city our size, we're honored and thrilled to have a star of her stature open up a concert tour here. You don't need me to tell you how much that has been anticipated."

At the Sorento Hotel, manager Howard Kennedy said lines formed around the arena when tickets went on sale,

a first for the Sudbury Community Arena. At a local record store, assistant manager Barbara Chaput said her phone had been ringing nonstop for weeks, all calls coming from people desperately seeking tickets.

At the Sheraton Hotel, where Shania stayed, guest services director Curt Deredin called it "an outstanding opportunity" for Sudbury, and the most prestigious moment in the hotel's history.

Because it was the first major concert since Shania had become the biggest-selling female artist in country music history—as well as one of the hottest performers in all of pop culture—the singer thought staging it near her hometown would remind the media how far she had come to reach this pinnacle.

At the same time, the media would arrive *en masse* to see firsthand if this comely star actually had any talent once she stepped outside of the gloss and magic of the recording studio.

Because her recordings owned a slick and carefully processed sheen, and because her videos focused on her dark beauty and shapely body, many critics had questioned the depth of her talent.

The fact that she decided not to tour as her breakthrough album, *The Woman in Me*, was setting sales records only gave more ammunition to those who suggested that she was a prefabricated construction masterminded by her husband, rock producer Robert John "Mutt" Lange.

One of the most successful record crafters in the history of modern pop music, Lange had worked wonders with such diverse artists as AC/DC, Bryan Adams, Billy Ocean, Def Leppard, The Cars, Michael Bolton, and Foreigner. With each act, he'd helped craft landmark pop albums that all sold in the multiple millions.

But to skeptics, Shania had become his greatest creation. Her 1993 debut album, recorded before Lange entered her life, barely sold at all. Other than a couple of videos that aired periodically on Country Music Television, Shania's self-titled debut was ignored by the country establishment. Then she married Lange, and her next album topped ten million in sales.

All during these years, hardly anyone had seen her perform. Few knew of the years of grueling nightclub shows or of her acclaimed headlining performances at a top Canadian resort. In America, she went from being ignored to being adored because of one album, and that album bore the name of one of the most successful record-makers in rock history.

Finally, after years of refusing to perform, her first tour of the arenas of North America would provide her with the opportunity to prove once and for all whether she could carry a tune live and whether she could communicate with an audience and entertain the fans she'd gathered with her hit songs.

Could she or couldn't she? She chose the comfort of home to answer that lingering question.

From the initial planning meetings, Shania made it clear to everyone involved what her show would be like.

"It's going to be high energy," she said. "It's going to be very dynamic. The music's going to be more exciting than how you hear it on the album. There's not going to be any elaborate props, and the set itself won't be hydraulic or anything like that. It's going to be about lights and sound and performance. I want it to be about performance as opposed to about the set."

In other words, she didn't want anyone accusing her of camouflaging her talent behind a flashy, multi-media stage production. There would be fireworks, but it wouldn't be tightly choreographed, or based on props or technological tricks. The singer wanted to make sure she proved her critics wrong, once and for all. And she wanted to make sure she communicated with the audience; that she created an air of intimacy instead of acting distant and aloof.

Every chance she got, Shania made it clear she was ready. She wasn't nervous, she said. Far from it. She was excited about the opportunity to finally get back onstage, her true performance home.

"I can't wait," she said. "I'm more anxious just because I haven't really had the opportunity to feel the audience's response. That's the thing I'm missing the most, to really feel the impact from the people, from the fans. As high as the numbers are in sales and things like that, they're just numbers to me. I can't really relate; it's too indirect. There's a void for me, and I want to see people respond to my music, live. Just to get out there and just, I don't know, vent. Just get out there and physically put myself into my music . . . I can't wait for it."

The support existed behind-the-scenes, too. Her manager, Jon Landau, said on the day before the show, "She works her butt off. She's very results-oriented, no-nonsense. She's going to blow a lot of people away."

Her husband was along for emotional support. But other than making sure the sound system worked well, he kept out of the limelight. When the press asked Shania if he would be in the wings, she shrugged and lied, saying she wasn't sure if he was coming. Lange notoriously protects his privacy, and she knew better than to tip off reporters that he was in attendance.

In Canada, especially, a quote from Lange or, even more importantly, a photo had been a high priority since the couple's marriage more than four years earlier. Even at the wedding, Lange refused to pose for photos, for fear they'd end up in the hands of some publication. He wanted nothing to do with the press or with any sort of publicity.

So when asked, Twain said her husband, a soccer fanatic, was thinking about traveling to Paris for the World Cup finals. She understood his need for privacy and to stay out of the glare of the world's media.

However, the day of the show, Lange lingered around the enormous soundboard situated near the back of the arena floor. He tweaked the sound, turning knobs and making last-minute adjustments.

"We've worked hard putting it together, but what I'm really interested in seeing is how the people react," Lange told a Canadian newspaper reporter who spotted him on the arena floor the evening of the concert. "That will be the barometer."

Other than that, Lange said, "the biggest concern for us is the sound. In a smaller arena like this, sound is always a bit of a lottery; you just never know."

For any big tour, a first show also gives a chance to work out some kinks. But George Travis, production manager for Shania's tour, felt confident going into Sudbury. A veteran who had worked on world tours with Bruce Springsteen, Madonna, and Mariah Carey, Travis told reporters he felt calm at a time when he usually would be scrambling because of last-minute details.

"What Shania has done is allowed us to go out and get all the very best people in order to put on a first-class show," Travis said. "We've got the best in the business; they've all got major experience with a host of top tours and artists."

As the starting hour for the show grew near, and as the arena filled to a capacity of slightly more than 5,000 people, the buzz in the air was electrifying. Leahy, a Canadian family band that blends Celtic and folk music into a *Riverdance*-style stage show, opened with a high-energy performance featuring fiddle-driven instrumentals and high-step folk dancing.

After they left the stage, Shania didn't keep them waiting long. Once the muscular couriers delivered her to the stage, Shania joined her band in moving vigorously to the opening chords of her song, "Man, I Feel Like a Woman."

Running across the stage as if warming up for a workout, beaming with high-watt charisma and extending her finger skyward, she shouted, "Are you ready, Sudbury?" The crowd answered with a deafening cheer, and the hometown hero smiled brilliantly and added, "Let's go, Sudbury!" Then she started the first song of the most important concert tour of her life.

After the song, which celebrates how wonderful it is to be alive and female, Shania breathily told the crowd, "I feel great! I've been waiting so long for this day and now it's finally here! I feel pumped!"

The crowd remained on its feet, never wavering in its noisy response. As wave after wave of cheers washed over her, she shook her long brown locks and shouted, "We're just getting started, Sudbury. I've got a lot of energy to burn."

The next day, in reviews across Canada and stretching as far as the daily *Tennessean* in Nashville, the comments were glowing. "OK, her detractors can now stop questioning Shania's singing ability," a Canadian critic wrote to lead his review.

Four months later, Shania would tackle the second-most important performance of the tour. It opened much the same way, except this time she didn't start with the chariot entrance. Perhaps that's because in Nashville, Shania still hadn't quite received the royal reception her record sales would seem to garner.

Still, on a warm and clear night in late September, she came onstage to a deafeningly positive reception in the capital of country music. "Are you ready, Nashville?!," she screamed, echoing the introduction of her first concert tour.

The crowd of more than 15,700 packed inside the sold-out Nashville Arena screamed its ecstatic response. The city where she'd struggled for acceptance, the only city where pockets of resistance to Shania-mania still held, had given her the answer she wanted.

If Shania still had something to prove, it was in Music City, USA. It's the town in which she launched her career. But it's also the town that still denied giving her any major awards, still whispered questions about her talent, still snickered and cracked jokes about her brash style and her fresh, forward-moving interpretation of modern country music.

Two nights prior to her concert, Shania left the Country Music Association Awards show without a single trophy. Considered by most music industry insiders to be the most prestigious night of honors in her musical genre of choice, the CMA Awards only nominated her for one major award, Album of the Year, for her *Come on Over* collection.

By far, her hit-filled album had been the best-selling and most-talked-about package of the year. Yet the award was given to Tim McGraw for his album *Everywhere*, which hadn't sold half as many as Shania's, even though it had been on the market twice as long.

To add insult to perfidy, when she opened the CMA show with a rousing, fireworks-filled version of her hit

"Honey, I'm Home," the industry-packed crowd responded with lackluster applause. After the song, CMA show host Vince Gill walked out on camera with his fingers in his ears and wisecracked that maybe the song should be called, "Honey, I'm Deaf," drawing a loud round of laughter from the Nashville insiders in the crowd. "Man, that was loud!" Gill said.

It was not much of a welcome for the person who had done the most to keep country music in the public eye during an otherwise drab period.

So, two nights later, when Shania bounced onstage at the Nashville Arena and asked, "Are you ready, Nashville?" it could be taken as more than a standard concert question.

Indeed, it could be the ongoing theme of her relationship with the home of country music: Nashville, are you ready for Shania Twain? The rest of the world has embraced her—the Canadian Country Music Awards had just given her a bevy of major awards two weeks earlier. So, why hasn't Music City, USA?

On this night, on this stage, in front of this crowd, all those doubts were cast aside. "Finally, I'm here with the tour in Nashville," she beamed. "It feels really wonderful."

At least inside the Nashville Arena, Shania has triumphed. For more than ninety minutes, the crowd stayed on its feet, waving banners with her name on it, throwing flowers onstage, shouting how much they love her. In response, Shania gave them all she had.

"I'm proud that I'm able to bring you a show in which

I do all of my own songs," she said, a reference to her reason for not touring until now. "Thanks for supporting my records without a tour."

In the end, the crowd stood and cheered until she returned to the stage. As far as the city's rank and file, she was every bit the star the rest of the world thought she was. How that resonated within the corridors of the Nashville music industry isn't yet known.

The day before the Nashville Arena show, one of the city's most visible entertainment agencies, Broadcast Music Inc., tried to assure Shania that Nashville was proud of her.

Roger Sovine, executive vice president at BMI, introduced Shania by announcing that the broadcast of the CMA Awards the previous evening had been the most watched show in its timeslot.

"I think a lot of it had to do with Shania Twain and that great opening number," said Sovine, whose company represents songwriters by tracking performances of copyrighted songs, then collecting and dispensing royalty payments to its members.

Another award to Shania was for her entry into the BMI "Million-Airs" club, given when a song has been played on radio stations more than a million times. Shania's song "Whose Bed Have Your Boots Been Under?" received the honor—quite an achievement, considering the song only went as high as number 15 on the country singles chart when it was originally released.

BMI President Frances Preston presented Shania

with the second honor. "It's a great accomplishment for such a young person to win an award like this, which usually takes many, many years to achieve," Preston said. "She should have all of our applause and praise."

Shania then stepped to the stage, smiling modestly and thanking everyone. "This is wonderful, all these treats and surprises," she said. "I don't know what else to say, this is just so wonderful."

Behind her, the cluster of tall buildings that made up the downtown Nashville skyline glistened in the early evening sun, a light breeze blowing across the fourth-floor terrace where the celebration took place.

Luke Lewis, the president of Mercury Nashville, grabbed a chance to add to the praise being showered on Shania. "Everybody from Nashville should be proud," he said of the singer's success. "All of the music on this album was made here, and we should be overjoyed at the success this woman has achieved."

Lewis's words seemed unusual. Instead of simply underlining the accomplishments of his singer, he seemed to be speaking directly to those in Nashville who continued to bad-mouth the successful country singer from Canada.

On a more personal note, Lewis told Shania, "The last six years have been the most gratifying of my career. I've realized my dreams, and a large part of the thanks for that goes to Shania Twain."

The BMI ceremony seemed to try to turn Shania away from the disappointment of the CMA Awards and toward the excitement of her sold-out show the following evening. Judging from the reaction at the concert, the week seemed to end on a high note for the singer. She and her supporters probably hoped the momentum within the city's music industry had finally turned in her favor.

Initially, the reaction to the show seemed positive. Respected music journalist Jay Orr of the daily *Tennessean* wrote that the show "put a big ol' exclamation point at the end of Country Music Week in Nashville." The concert, Orr said, took a giant leap beyond that of any of her contemporaries—a big statement from Orr, who had been very vocal in his support of Garth Brooks over the years.

At the same time, Shania's concert remained rooted in the family values that so often characterize country music shows, he wrote, adding, "Any doubts that she could support her top-selling albums with a state-of-the-art show were erased last night."

Only a few weeks earlier, when Shania appeared on the cover of *Rolling Stone* magazine, a gossip columnist in the *Tennessean* wrote that many women on Music Row told him that "her eyes look dead."

Considering that Shania was the first country music artist to appear on the cover of the magazine since Dolly Parton in 1980, the Shania story should have been deemed a triumph by the country music industry. That it instead sparked a flurry of catty comments spoke volumes about how industry insiders still view Shania with suspicion.

After the Nashville concert, the same *Tennessean* columnist who wrote about the *Rolling Stone* article also counteracted Orr's review by bad-mouthing the concert. Brad Schmidt, a daily gossip columnist for the paper, provided this synopsis of Shania's show: "What if Mary Poppins wore tight vinyl pants and a top that showed her belly?"

Shania's athletic, sexy image didn't fit with the moments when she brought kids onstage and spoke about poverty, spousal abuse, and feeding young children, he said. He thought her presentation might prove especially confusing to the very youngsters to whom she reached out.

"Here's this sexy singer who markets herself as a sexy singer bringing children onto the stage with her and reading kids' fan mail in the middle of her show," Schmidt wrote.

He described it as "two shows in one: a sexy, high energy funfest that screeched to a halt when her Barney family show was thrown in the middle." She was effective at both roles, he said, but "the mistake was mixing them together."

Schmidt ended his column by asking for comments. He got them. "Right now, just because a female is thin, and you can see some of her skin, you are looking at her as a sex object," a reader wrote. "When you are able to look at her as a person, it won't bother you that she hugs a child. When you can see the world in a healthy and correct way, your popularity with women will magnify."

Others saw this dual image in a better light. In a musical guide designed for parents, *Entertainment Weekly* called Shania "Wynonna with attitude," saying she was "a little bit country, a little bit rock 'n' roll." Her message of "find your self-esteem and be forever free to dream" was empowering, the magazine said. However, like Schmidt, the magazine wondered if that message was diluted with her come-hither poses.

So Shania left Nashville with mixed messages—a common occurrence since her multimillion breakthrough. Even with the BMI event, even with the sold-out concert, she went home without a CMA award—the only true sanction the entire Nashville music industry gives to country music artists.

"People in Nashville will not give her an inch," said one top Nashville record-company executive. "It's the same with Garth. It's like, 'How dare these two people come along and be successful when we didn't shape them? How dare Mutt Lange make good records!' There's so much resentment. But anyway, I don't think she and her people give a shit about dominating country music. They're shooting for a real, real big career, like a Madonna or a Barbra Streisand career. In the meantime though, we in Nashville are going to clone her any which way we can—already every girl act signed better have good stomach muscles. And then, of course, we're going to dump on her any moment we can."

Shania says she doesn't care about her naysayers—at least that's what she says in public. As long as people are buying her albums, she knows she has the support of those who matter. "It's the fans who have kept all this momentum going," she said. "I think the country music industry is refreshed by this. There may be some people who don't get it, but that's OK. They don't have to get it, as long as the fans do."

Chapter Two

From a Faraway Place

TIMMINS, ONTARIO, IS NOT A GLAMOROUS PLACE. A gold-mining outpost, it sits at the northern edge of civilization in North America, a flat landscape of stark pines and beautiful, clear waterways. It's a sprawling, thinly populated city that covers an enormous amount of land for its population of 47,500. Its primary reason for being is to provide gold ore and timber for wealthier, more populated places; for that reason, it's a place populated by pioneers, roustabouts, and those with nowhere else to run.

Far from any major city, it draws those who need

work, outdoorsmen who like to hunt and ice fish, and those who like a quiet, low-key life. "Most people who grow up here leave," says a childhood acquaintance of Shania, who pointed out that most of the singer's peers have left town, just as the singer did.

Still, Timmins isn't without its Chamber of Commerce-style pride. "The City with a Heart of Gold," a slogan local boosters have bestowed upon the town, transforms the city's primary economic base, gold mining, into a cheerful and optimistic statement of community pride. In the winter, though, that golden heart can get awfully cold: Temperatures fall as low as minus-forty degrees in winter.

Shania has always considered Timmins her hometown, and that's what she told record company image makers when preparing for the issuance of her first album. Indeed, she grew up in the remote city, moving there with her mother and older sister when she was two years old. In truth, though, she was born in Windsor, Ontario—a suburban city in Southern Ontario that's far closer to urban Toronto than to the remote flatlands of Timmins.

Shania's father worked hard and dreamed huge, but he never earned much. He logged timber for money, and he worked as a miner only when desperate. He focused on prospecting, hoping for the big score. Mostly, though, his family went hungry, barely paying bills and often skipping meals. When milk was brought into the house, it was levied out in exact proportions. Some nights meals existed only of milk, bread, and sugar, warmed and stirred in a pot to simulate porridge; at other times, family members received one potato a piece for the day's food.

To augment the meager table offerings, Jerry Twain often went into the woods to hunt game, both by trap and by rifle. He taught his children to help hunt as well, with the hard-driven Shania his favorite and most enthusiastic assistant. "My father taught us to kill our own food," she has said. "My job was to set the rabbit snares."

School could be tough for her. She often got by on lunches of sliced bread, with two pieces coated inside with mustard or mayonnaise to suggest a sandwich. Others ate ham and roast beef, chips, and big, shiny, juicy fruit. Shania tried not to react, taking great pains to camouflage her lack of a meal so that the teachers didn't get upset.

She worried obsessively that she'd be taken away from her family because of the poverty. When she worried, it was more for her parents than for herself. She knew how proud they were, and she didn't want them embarrassed by any social-service inquiries. Even though she was often gravely hungry, she never complained, never asked for handouts, never begged for any leftovers from friends, and never tried to convince anyone to share. She kept quiet and to herself.

"I was the kid that always went to school without a lunch," she said. While "always" is an exaggeration, family members and those who knew her then say that her family went through long periods where they got by on a thread of a shoestring.

"I'd judge other kids' wealth by their lunches," Shania would say later, laughing now at what must have been difficult then. "If a kid had baked goods, that was like, 'Oh, they must be rich.' "

As she recalls now, her childhood was difficult, but she harbors no bitterness. "I don't look at it as a bad thing at all," she said. "I don't regret my childhood. Learning to make mustard sandwiches was something just to get me through the embarrassment, to help me avoid humiliation."

When someone did find out, she'd argue with them, refusing to admit her circumstances. Later in life, when telling the story, if someone remarked about how sad or deprived she must have been as a child, she'd quickly correct them, telling them it wasn't sad, nor was it difficult, nor did she feel deprived.

Through it all, she's never once criticized or even hinted at bad feelings toward her parents, despite what she went through. She's only expressed deep, abiding love and respect for them. She has always said that she understood that they did their best, that her father had dreams as well as immense pride. Even though they could have received government or community assistance, they did not. "It was a pride thing," she said. "I respect him for that. I don't feel bad for myself, not even for a second."

Understandably, her parents did feel bad about it, especially for the children. Close-knit and private, they shared love but little else. When times were tough,

Sharon Twain would fall into deep depressions, unable to cope with the guilt she felt for the Twains' inability to provide for their children as she thought proper. She tried her best, planting gardens in the spring and washing clothes by hand to save on laundry and water bills, but it was a struggle.

For all the emotional weight involved, Shania never cried when talking about her past. "Tough times," she would remark, but if she felt any emotion when discussing it, she never showed it.

Besides love, her parents invested in her dreams and gave her confidence. They truly believed in the talent Shania displayed at a young age. By three years old, she surprised her family with her vocal ability. Not only could she sing on key, with a light vibrato, but she also showed a mastery of the difficult trick of harmony singing.

In first grade, Shania performed "Take Me Home, Country Roads," at the time a massive radio hit for John Denver (another singer who mixed country and pop with great success). By the age of eight, she could sing and play guitar with amazing proficiency. By age ten, she began writing her own songs.

"I liked to escape my personal life through my music," she would later say about childhood. "Music was all I ever did. I spent a lot of time in solitude with just my guitar, writing and singing away for hours. I would play 'til my fingers were bruised, and I loved it!"

Along the way, her mother started to think that her

daughter owned something very special, and that it could take their impoverished family to a better life than the one they endured.

"My mother lived for my career," Shania would later say. "We were extremely poor when I was a kid, and my mother was often depressed having five children and no food to feed them. She knew I was talented, and she lived with the hope that my abilities were my chance to do something special."

Shania inherited her love of music from her parents. Like many poor people, they turned to the radio and the occasional record to help them get through hard times, to bring moments of joy and lightness to a dreary and difficult life.

Her parents loved the stories and the realities of country music, and they liked the beauty of pop harmonies. There wasn't any of the darkness of hard rock or punk music in Shania's life, nor did she delve very deeply into dance music or rap.

As a child, the music her family turned up loud included songs of gruff defiance and hard-earned love by Waylon Jennings, Willie Nelson, and Johnny Paycheck, as well as songs about difficult times by Tammy Wynette and Dolly Parton. Along with that, they smiled and sang along with the Carpenters, the Mamas and the Papas, the Fifth Dimension, and the buoyant Motown music of the Supremes, the Temptations, Smokey Robinson and the Miracles, and Shania's favorite, Stevie Wonder.

She once said that the biggest dream she could imagine, the most wonderful thing in the world, would be to get a job as a background singer for Stevie Wonder. That would be the life, she thought when she was young.

Back then, Shania was too shy to dream of stardom. Later, she would say, her most extravagant thoughts were of writing songs for others, maybe singing in the background where she didn't attract attention to herself.

But her mom had other ideas. With her husband's support, Sharon Twain pushed her daughter to get out and perform in front of people. At first, she went to community centers, nursing homes, and hospital wards. Quickly, however, she graduated to nightclubs. Her parents would wait until 1 A.M., when liquor stopped being served and minors could be allowed inside. Then they'd haul their sleepy daughter through the doors and plant themselves as close to the stage as possible. If it was a first-time visit, they'd wait for a break to ask the band if their daughter could sing, or sometimes Jerry Twain would enter early to see if it was possible for his daughter to sing before deciding to bring his family out that late at night.

Once Shania became successful, she occasionally looked back at those late-night performances with bitterness. "I hated it," she told writer Dave Hoekstra of the *Chicago Sun-Times*. "I didn't feel like singing at that time of the night at all."

But she did it, with few complaints. And her parents, also early morning risers, persevered. Her mother worked in the kitchen at the Hotel Mattagami, now a run-down flophouse with strippers performing in its bar area—the sign outside reads "cold beer, hot women" on one side, while advertising table-dance specials on the other.

In those days, however, the Hotel Mattagami was a rundown but respectable place, with country and Top 40 songs played on the stage for the blue-collar crowd.

To get ready for an evening of performing, Sharon Twain would dress her young daughter in denim skirts and vests with buckskin fringe. At 1 A.M., most of the loggers and miners would be drunk, and smoke and stale beer filled the air. But the gritty Shania would stand up and belt out her songs, her tiny but forceful voice filling the room as she strummed a guitar nearly as big as she was. It was a tough, if not discerning, crowd, and the fact that she got up there night after night speaks volumes about what a determined child she must have been.

OFTEN, THE BAND WAS MORE THAN HAPPY TO LET go of a few songs amid a night of performing for five or more hours with few breaks. Shania, then known by her given name of Eilleen, became a fixture at several of the city's roughest nightspots, playing for hard-drinking miners, down-and-out loggers, and the semi-employed.

As Shania entered her teens, her parents began hauling her to Toronto for voice lessons, a grueling twenty-hour roundtrip drive from Timmins. The voice teacher occasionally found the young, precocious singer jobs in other cities as well.

Mary Bailey, a popular Canadian country singer in the '70s, will always remember the first time she saw Shania perform as a young girl. Standing in the spotlight, she held herself with poise and poured herself into an acoustic version of the Hank Williams' classic, "I'm so Lonesome I Could Cry."

"She was this little girl who got onstage with a guitar and just blew me away," recalled Bailey, who got far enough along in her career to release two singles on RCA Records before retiring from the stage. The first time she heard Shania, Bailey cried, struck by the ripe emotion this girl brought to this age-old standard.

At age sixteen, Shania joined the rock bank Longshot. David Hartt, the band's guitarist, heard the singer perform in a club and immediately invited her to audition for his band. "We wouldn't let her leave the audition until she promised to join the band," Hartt says. "There was such power in her voice. It was such an adult voice for someone so young."

Longshot was a popular band at high-school parties and community events, where the quintet performed covers of Pat Benatar, Journey, and REO Speedwagon. (During this time, she likely performed songs produced by her husband, including Foreigner's "Urgent," and AC/DC's "I Shook You All Night Long.")

Besides performing, Shania held other jobs to help out

at home. Like millions of other teens around the world, she worked at McDonald's, one of the first fast-food chains to set up in Timmins. She later worked at Sears, gaining a job in the difficult catalog department, which was ground-zero for anyone with complaints or questions. By all accounts, she was cheerful, helpful, and good at her job, remaining patient and poised when faced with angry adults.

Such jobs were similar to those held by other teens from struggling, hard-working households, but Shania's experience also extended beyond that.

By now, her father had added reforestation work to his list of self-employed jobs. He'd take on contracts to seed forest areas that had been decimated by lumber companies, planting seeds for the next generation of timber cutters. It was seasonal work, and her father took Shania along in the summers, teaching her to handle a chainsaw and other logging equipment. He also taught her to set a trap and shoot a rifle, so that she could help him in every level of his daily toils. As with her work serving Big Macs and facilitating catalog orders, she did what others might consider adult work without whining or complaining. She already was showing a resolve and a willingness to work hard, even when most youngsters resist such endeavors.

From all accounts, she also didn't rebel or party with her peers. She resisted drugs, which were popular among her friends, and she rarely drank to excess. But her love of music gave her a freedom and hipness that the hard-partying crowd embraced. Through music, the once-shy Shania found common ground with others.

Later in life, she would laugh about her knowledge of drugs, which she learned from being around those who indulged. She could identify blond and black hash, but she had never experienced the different highs the two forms provided. She never tried any of it. Maybe it was her work ethic, her ambition, or her steely individualism. Maybe playing in bars turned her off to inebriation. Maybe she was just wiser than the rest. But she didn't fall prey to the bad habits that engulf many young musicians.

To *Rolling Stone* magazine—once the bible of the counter-culture—she explained it this way: "I was so high on music, and the music was so good—Supertramp, Rush, and Pink Floyd. We're all going to see Pink Floyd, and I'm like, 'You guys want to put a few things on your tongue and do acid, you just go ahead.' Meanwhile, I probably looked high. I used to really rock out. I'd get people coming up to me saying, 'Do you do drugs or what?' I never did, but I looked like I did."

Maureen Yakabuski, Shania's twelfth grade English teacher, recalled that what stood out about the young, intense student was her determination. "She sang sometimes two or three nights a week and would come to class the next day," the teacher said. "She would always make a point of getting the work done and hand it in. She was a conscientious student, although music was the love of her life much more than English literature was."

Other classmates remember her as charismatic but

aloof. Some saw her as snobby, as if she considered herself better than them, but that's often the bane of every attractive but reserved teenager. Mostly her fellow students remember her drive, her ambition, and her single-minded concentration on music.

"Remember me when I'm famous and I'll remember you," she wrote in the yearbook of classmate Olaf Karl. It wasn't necessarily an empty boast. Many in Timmins thought Shania had the talent to become a popular performer. "We always knew she would amount to something," said David Hartt, her former bandmate.

To Shania, though, music owned two purposes: Performing allowed her to grow more at ease with herself and with others. But, to her, music was most important as a private escape. Whether listening intently to the radio or writing her own songs in her bedroom with her door locked, Shania developed a personal relationship with music, letting it transport her beyond her dismal surroundings.

Even though she grew quite comfortable onstage, she never grew very comfortable in her own skin in daily life. She especially felt awkward with her own body and her sexuality. She was painfully shy, and when her body developed feminine curves before most of her classmates, she tried to hide it. She also hated it when boys approached her or hounded her.

"I spent my whole youth hiding behind a tomboy image," Shania said. "I spent my whole youth trying to hide my figure. I wanted to stay the tomboy forever. I wanted to stay flat-chested forever. I didn't want the curves because of the attention it drew to me. It's like the better shape you were in and the more curves you had, the more you stood out. And you didn't want to stand out for that."

For that reason, Shania often wore three shirts and tight undergarments to flatten out her chest. Most of the other girls in her class also dressed in a way to hide their figures. Those who didn't paid the consequences.

"There was one girl in my school who didn't care," Shania recalled. "She had a figure very similar to mine. She was very curvy. We were in track and field together, and she just let it fly. She didn't care. She was being natural. And I remember what people thought of her at the time. I would never have been caught being thought of in that way, so I strapped myself down and made sure I wore layers and made sure that I was hidden as much as possible. I regret that now, and I admire (the other girl) for that. There was nothing wrong with that. She was being very natural, and it was everybody else that had the problem."

After graduation, Shania's mother contacted Mary Bailey, the Canadian country singer who had been so encouraging of her daughter when she was younger. By that time, Shania already had made her first trip to Nashville. A would-be manager had taken the seventeen-year-old girl to Nashville, but the brief visit didn't result in anything positive.

Not sure how to proceed with Shania's future, Sharon

asked Bailey if she would manager her daughter. Bailey, though inexperienced, agreed. She bought out the contract from the previous manager. Before long, she, too, took the young singer to Nashville. Once again, no one showed interest, even if Bailey got the youngster through a few more doors than her predecessor.

But Shania didn't seem to care then if Nashville didn't embrace her. She was more interested in pop and rock in those days anyway, Bailey said. Besides, in those years, few teen singers got any notice in Nashville, anyway.

As time passed, Bailey and Shania fell out of touch. The two soon let their contract slip by without renewal. Shania seemed content performing in the club circuit that extended from Timmins to Toronto.

One aspect people remember about the young Shania was her poise—she always seemed very centered, if quiet. But if she needed a reason to lose her bearings and her supreme confidence, it came in 1987. That's when her parents were suddenly and tragically removed from her life.

One afternoon, as Jerry and Sharon Twain returned from a business trip with their youngest son, Darryl, in the back seat, their Chevy Suburban was struck by a raging logging truck which had been fully loaded and speeding down the two-lane highway when it crossed the center line on a turn, and collided head-on with the family car. Both of her parents were killed instantly, and her brother miraculously survived with only minor injuries. Shania was twenty-one.

The young performer was in Toronto for a singing engagement when the accident occurred. She heard the news from her sister, Carrie, who is three years younger than Shania. As Carrie recalled, Shania immediately returned to Timmins. "I just remember pretty much saying what happened and hanging up the phone, and the next thing, she was sort of there."

For most anyone, the death of a parent can be a life-defining, life-changing moment. But to lose both parents in a tragic accident at such a young age can levy a nearly unimaginable emotional burden on someone, especially considering how close Shania was to her mother and father. For her, though, the burden was two-fold, for she was the one who assumed daily care for her younger siblings: eighteen-year-old Carrie, fourteen-year-old Mark, and thirteen-year-old Darryl.

Shania had to deal with the details of burying and mourning her parents as well as taking care of the children and their constant needs. She was forced to deal with the estate, taxes, and the other minutiae of death and continuance. She moved back into her family's home and took care of her brothers, thrown back into the poverty that she and her family had left behind in recent years.

"At the time, I thought, 'I don't have time to grieve for myself,'" she told a columnist for *USA Weekend* in 1996. "But taking care of my siblings was a blessing in disguise. It was a total distraction from grief."

Two years later, in 1998, she would tell *Rolling Stone*, "I became very hard for quite a long time. Just nobody could do anything to even remotely hurt me. I was so numb. Nothing penetrated. It was a very difficult time. But boy, oh boy, did I ever get strong."

Among those she called on for help was her old friend and mentor, Mary Bailey. Shania worried that her dreams of making her way in music were over; she figured she needed to get a steady job and concentrate on premature parenthood.

Bailey, a parent of two, encouraged her not to give up her aspirations. The veteran singer suggested that perhaps Shania could find steady work as a performer at one location, so she could set a steady schedule and receive a regular paycheck.

Among the auditions Mary arranged for the young woman included one for a position at the Deerhurst Resort, a popular tourist spot 150 miles north of Toronto. Shania got the job, which allowed her to sing full-time without traveling, as well as providing her with a steady income far beyond what she'd ever earned before. It turned out to be one of the most important connections of her life.

It also proved to be a near-perfect situation: She gained the opportunity to perform a variety of music on a daily basis, entertaining travelers rather than drunks. The work also allowed her to further develop her own stage persona and to grow much more comfortable onstage.

"That's where my biggest development as a performer really took place," she said. "First, I was able to overcome a lot of the inhibitions I had left about performing.

It's easy to get up and sing in a country bar, where it's just a party, but when you're in front of a lot of people and you're essentially on a pedestal and everyone stops to listen, you've got to start *performing*. Secondly, I got to work with some great professionals and learn a lot about staging, choreography, and production. I got a really good taste of what I'm doing now."

Just as importantly, she provided a stable environment for her younger brothers. At ages thirteen and fourteen, they were fairly independent. Still, Shania gave them a good home, buying a house near Deerhurst and a reliable pickup truck.

Shania soon grew into a main attraction at Deerhurst. The resort presented a variety of shows in its three performance halls, offering country music, pop hits, and a Broadway-style revue. Shania spent time performing all of the styles. While the singer was glad to move out of the hard-drinking bars of Northern Ontario, the Deerhurst revelers conferred upon her a different kind of challenge. Since they were vacationers, she had no chance of building up a regular audience. Each night, she was expected to win over a new set of strangers. It taught her to communicate with an audience, to work hard at entertaining as well as singing.

Even with a grueling nightly schedule, Shania more than fulfilled her duties as guardian of her school-age brothers. She took them to school each morning and picked them up each afternoon. She attended parent-teacher meetings, drove them to dances and sporting events, and tried to steer them right and keep them out of trouble.

She wasn't always the perfect guardian—which was understandable, considering the daunting responsibilities she had taken on. "There were times I was angry at life, and I'd take it out on them," she said. "But I think they understood my grief. We got through it together."

But they made it. After three years at Deerhurst, as the boys graduated in successive years, Shania went through the same experiences any mother felt.

When the boys moved away on their own, she said she at first "felt like a forty-five-year-old woman whose kids had gone away to college." But once they were gone, she realized she now had a freedom that she didn't have when she was caring for her brothers. "I was like, 'Wow!' I had all this time on my hands. I didn't have to cook and clean for anybody. Didn't have to pay any bills but mine. Didn't have to go to school meetings. Didn't have to pick them up after work and take them to teen dances. Drive 'em here. Drive 'em there. It was like, 'I'm free!' I said, 'Now what am I gonna do with my new life? I decided I wanted to go for it!'"

Chapter Three

On My Way

MEANWHILE, MARY BAILEY AND SHANIA HAD formed a mother-daughter relationship of sorts. Bailey had always believed strongly in the talent and potential of Shania, who she not only admired, but loved. The veteran entertainer once again assumed management of the young Shania, only now she looked upon her more as a loved one than a client.

Bailey, with money from her family's bank account, invested heavily in her young protégé. She wanted everything about Shania to be as professional and as glamorous as possible. From stage clothes to sound equipment, to band members to transportation, Bailey made sure the singer came across as a first-class act. She showcased Shania in the best possible light, so that her talent wasn't hindered in any way.

Robert Kasner, Bailey's son, said their family sacrificed so that his mother could give everything she could to her young, fledgling starlet. "My dad was making his money and my mom was spending it on this dream," Kasner said. "Everything had to be perfect before she went out with Shania."

Bailey's guidance proved invaluable in helping Shania prepare to climb to the next level in her career. Through friends, the manager sent a cassette tape of Shania's music to a high-powered Nashville attorney, Dick Frank, who represented several country music stars. Frank had a good relationship with many of the business leaders on Nashville's famed Music Row.

Frank liked what he heard on Shania's tape. He set up a trip to Deerhurst, so he could see a performance by the talented woman, then twenty-six and still known as Eilleen Twain.

At Deerhurst, Frank enjoyed what he saw: an exuberant woman with striking beauty, great poise, a well-developed stage presence, and a strong, clear vocal style.

Frank then contacted his friend Norro Wilson, a veteran Nashville producer. Wilson had been a Music Row fixture for more than three decades, and was one of the few veteran country producers to make the transition into the '90s.

Originally a performer and songwriter—his hits include Charlie Rich's classic "(Did You Happen to See) The Most Beautiful Girl in the World"—Wilson made his mark by producing hit albums for George Jones and Tammy Wynette, as well as such contemporary performers as Mindy McCready, Sara Evans, and Sammy Kershaw.

Wilson listened to Shania's tape. Taking into account what the reliable attorney told him about her live performance and her attractive presence, he agreed to meet with her. Shania, with her manager, flew to Nashville, and she and Wilson quickly hit it off. The producer is a warm, large man with a quick, self-deprecating wit, and Shania liked him from the start.

Wilson took the young Canadian into a Nashville recording studio, a daunting environment, even for an experienced stage singer. The cold, impersonal nature of a recording studio is vastly different than singing into a microphone in front of a live band and a noisy crowd. Every flaw becomes magnified, every insecurity multiplied. For an innately shy woman like Shania, the pressure can bring out a self-conscious awkwardness that makes it hard to relax and do one's best. Shania had been in a recording studio before, but never under these circumstances, never with her whole future on the line.

Wilson could see she was nervous, even though Shania tried to hide it rather than admitting it. So Wilson worked to relax her, cracking jokes, talking casually and intimately. He tried to make the event seem routine, like it wasn't such a big deal.

"Just want to get some things down on tape here," he told her. "I already know you're good. I can hear that. I want to try a few things with you, see what suits you best."

In the end, the two recorded three new songs with Shania. He took the finished tape to Buddy Cannon, an artists-and-repertoire executive at Mercury Records. Cannon found the singer enchanting, and passed the tape and a strong recommendation to Harold Shedd, then head of the Nashville division of Mercury Records.

A decade earlier, Shedd had discovered the biggest country band of all time, Alabama, and had produced all of their initial ground-breaking hits. He also had produced award-winning songs in the 1980s with singer K. T. Oslin, and he'd discovered such hot country singers as Billy Ray Cyrus, Sammy Kershaw, Terri Clark, and Toby Keith.

Harold was mightily impressed with Shania, believing she had a youthful appeal as well as a strong, if not outstanding, voice. He signed her to Mercury Records in 1991 and agreed to work with Wilson in producing her first album.

Shedd made one suggestion: He didn't like the name Eilleen Twain. He proposed she come up with another stage name. The singer remembered a woman she knew while at the Deerhurst Resort who had an Indian name,

"Shania." It was an Ojibwa name, which meant it connected with the ancestry of her stepfather. Moreover, in
the Ojibwa language, the name meant, "I'm on my way!"

That was certainly how Eilleen Twain felt at the moment. So, from that point on, the name Eilleen melted
away, only to be spoken by family members and those
few who remembered her in Timmins and in Huntsville,
at the Deerhurst Resort. Everyone else would know her
as Shania.

Shedd set a date for recording the album, scheduling it
to begin after he finished work on an album by another
new artist he had just signed named Billy Ray Cyrus.
(Among the songs recorded on that album include "Achy
Breaky Heart," the biggest hit single in country music in
the '90s.)

As preparations for beginning Shania's first album
moved along, the two powerful men guiding her career at
that point plugged Shania into the Nashville system.
Shania met with publicists, image consultants, and booking agents. She also started co-writing songs with leading
Music Row songwriters, including Kent Robbins, who
had scored numerous hits by the likes of the Judds, John
Anderson, and Ronnie Milsap.

Shedd and Wilson also gathered songs from the
biggest and most successful music publishing houses.
With a box full of tapes of songs from various writers, the
two men sat down with the singer to go through the material. As they listened, the producers made suggestions
on which songs might own the best opportunity to get

played on country radio, the most important step in establishing a new country star.

They also set her up with the best studio musicians they could recruit: Drummer Larrie Londin had played with Elvis Presley, the Everly Brothers, Chet Atkins, and Mark Knopfler; guitarist Reggie Young had played with Waylon Jennings, Jimmy Buffett, and Johnny Cash. All of the musicians—from bassist Glen Worf to acoustic guitarist Billy Joe Walker to steel guitarist Sonny Garrish—were ranked among the best at what they did.

Shania was excited, at least at first. It happened so fast it seemed. Despite all her trips to Nashville, despite all the years of dreaming and scheming and playing any place that would have her, she felt almost unprepared for what was happening.

From the day she met Dick Frank to the time she went into the studio encompassed only a matter of months. Elated with each step, she nonetheless felt rushed, as if the producers didn't take enough time to get to know her before putting her in front of the microphone.

Wilson, especially, sensed Shania's unease and went out of his way to try and make her comfortable in Nashville. Some producers only see their artists in a few specially arranged meetings to go over songs and musical ideas, then hook up with them in the studio. But Wilson checked on Shania regularly, making sure she was OK, giving her encouragement about the future. He even took her with him to the annual BMI country awards dinner, one of the hottest tickets and most prestigious events in the Nashville music community.

That night, Shania was walking on stars. She attended the awards dressed in an elegant gown, maintaining a classy poise amid all the stars and all the glamour that Nashville can stir.

For all of his attention and concern, though, Shania felt left out of the most important part of the process for her—that is, choosing songs. The producers weren't giving her much input into what songs she would record, and it began to eat at her.

The turning point came when she realized they weren't interested in the incredible amount of songs she'd written over the years. That truly bothered Shania. She loved to write, and she thought her songs said something new, something fresh. They represented her point of view and signified who she was.

Shania realized that plenty of others could sing as well as she. And plenty of them are beautiful, shapely women, many of whom could perform well onstage. But no one wrote songs quite like she did, she thought.

As the recording time neared, Shania began to feel as though she'd been put upon a conveyor belt, as if she was being shaped to sound like other country singers instead of sounding like herself.

She protested, at least a little. She could see the producers lining up songs by outsider writers, songs by such leading Nashville songwriters as Gretchen Peters, Skip Ewing, and Mike Reid. But they weren't her songs.

Shedd and Wilson tried to soothe her hurt feelings. Her songs were good, very good in fact. But they were different, and country radio often was slow to accept something different.

In the modern record world, a performer sometimes only had one chance to get a foothold. The songs they chose, she was told, were written to fit the country-radio format. She'd own a much better chance at establishing herself if she followed the formula.

Once established, once she had the attention of radio programmers and country fans, she could begin to exert more of her own personality and her own style. Radio would be more receptive to her own songs once she'd proven that fans liked her.

Shania went along with the plan, despite her doubts. She really didn't have a choice. If she protested, Mercury Records had plenty of other wannabe stars waiting in line who would do exactly as told. She didn't want to seem ungrateful for the opportunity.

She did contribute one song to her first album, one that she co-wrote with Kent Robbins. "God Ain't Gonna Getcha for That" featured a theme Shania would later expand upon, once she got the chance to create her own music.

The song tells of a young woman in a honky tonk who spies a guy sitting quietly in a corner, detached from the music and the dancing revelers. The woman approaches the fellow, asks if she can "buy him a brew," and wryly points out that it's OK to loosen up and have a good time, that "God ain't gonna getcha for that."

That idea, of a woman taking the lead and being more aggressive than the man in the song, is just the kind of role reversal Shania loves to use in her songs. Similarly, "God Ain't Gonna Getcha for That" features sly humor and exaggerated come-ons—two other themes that would later flower in several of Shania's best-loved songs.

In the end, Shania settled for what others said would be best for her. It would be the last time she relied on advice from executives rather than following her own instincts.

Chapter Four

Mercury Rising

MERCURY RECORDS, THE COMPANY TO WHICH SHANIA had staked her future, underwent a drastic change before the Canadian's first record came out. After she'd finished recording her songs, but before anyone else had a chance to hear them, Mercury Records realigned its Nashville operations.

A&M Records, a well-established company based in Los Angeles, was now a part of the Polygram Record Group, as was Mercury Nashville. A&M wanted to establish a presence in Nashville and in country music, and

Polygram executives in Los Angeles tabbed Harold Shedd to start up and manage the new company.

At Mercury Nashville, Polygram brought in an outsider, Luke Lewis, who had spent most of his life running the important distribution arms of major record companies, first at CBS Records and later for MCA/Universal. Lewis, though not a creative record man like Harold Shedd, loved music with a passion. He also had different ideas than Harold on how to manage artists and on how to run a record company.

Shania worried that she might be hurt by the fact that the man responsible for bringing her to the company was no longer associated with her success. Lewis might be more likely to want to build his own success story at the company, rather to continue a plan that would reflect well on Shedd rather than on himself.

However, for the most part, the record company stuck to the plans originally set in motion by Shedd. Mercury thought the best way to establish Shania would be to exploit the unusual aspects of Shania's heritage: Her rural Canadian upbringing, her Native-American cultural ties, her parents' dedication to getting her career started at an early age, her experience in logging and prospecting, even the death of her parents—though, by Shania's insistence, this aspect was downplayed while the others were emphasized.

Her first record company biography, a three-page summary of her life to that point, served as her introduction to radio programmers, booking agents, retail executives, and the press. It opened by stating, "It would be hard to imagine two more fundamentally different worlds than those in which Shania Twain has lived. Shania spent much of her late teens and early adulthood alternating between leading a thirteen-man forest crew deep in Canada's northern woods, where she grew up, and entertaining in some of the most glamorous resorts and nightspots of the Toronto region."

Shania's opening quote was somewhat duplicitous. Everyone who had ever crossed her path would have quickly learned of her overwhelming obsession with music and performing. All of her family, friends, classmates, and co-workers knew what she was and what she wanted to be. She had even been pictured in her Timmins High yearbook singing a song—which is the way most of her peers thought of her.

For some reason, Shania wanted people to think otherwise. "The funny thing is," she said in the bio, "when I'm in the music world, people can't believe I've ever lived such a rustic life. And people from back home for the most part don't know about the other life I've had. I've never talked about it. They're going to be really shocked when they see this album."

However, the only shock likely felt by old friends in Timmins was seeing that she had changed her name from Eilleen to Shania. Otherwise, anyone she'd met would not at all be surprised to see her on an album cover. It was something many of them expected, and even those naysayers who never thought she would make it knew it was what she wanted.

Though later she would claim she was forced against her judgment to record the songs in that style, at the time she described it much differently. Indeed, when her first album came out, she described it to interviewers in much the same way she would describe her next two albums, which were made under entirely different circumstances.

"The album is very diverse, but all of it is me," she said, a theme she would repeat for years to come, even though her music would never again sound like it did on her 1993 debut. "I've always sung country, but it didn't take me long as a teenager to begin exploring different kinds of music. I had a lot of classical vocal lessons that let me realize the range I had and the fun I could have with my voice, so I explored everything from rock and R&B to Christian music, and I tried to bring all those elements into my writing as that developed."

Though she barely mentioned how impoverished the Twains were, she generously credited her parents for their diligence in pushing her to perform as much and as well as possible. For some reason, however, she continued to pound the issue that her musical life was kept secret from her peers. In truth, of course, everyone at her high school—administrators, teachers, students, even those she didn't know—were aware that she sang at carnivals, fairs, festivals, and in local bars.

"They never knew this side of me," Shania said in her

bio. "I've always been very quiet about myself that way. Even my schoolmates never knew I was a singer. It was just something I did for myself, something I was very private about."

That's less than truthful, of course. But, for some reason, Shania felt a need to make up a story to illustrate this elaborate fabrication.

Her bio went on: "A friend of mine in high school asked me once, 'Is it true that you play in a band at night, and that you went to do *The Tommy Hunter Show* in Toronto?'"

In truth, Shania didn't sing on the *The Tommy Hunter Show*, a popular television variety series in Canada in the 1980s, until several years after she graduated from high school.

While promoting her first album, she exaggerated other aspects of her life as well. While she did on occasion accompany her father on reforestation projects, she turned this seed into a fantastic, but false, story about the double-life she purports to have lived.

"From spring through fall I'd work with my father in the bush," the bio continues. "I was a foreman with a thirteen-man crew, many of whom were Indians. I'd run the crew, and we'd plant millions of trees through the summer. We'd get up between four and six in the morning, live on beans, bread, and tea, walk up to an hour to the site, and work there all day with no shelter in rain, snow, or sunshine, in the middle of the bush, hours from civilization. I did that for five years. It was very hard work, but I loved it. Then, after a summer of northern exposure, from the treacherous June blackflies to an August hailstorm, I'd go back to Toronto and slip into my sequined gown again. I come from two completely different worlds, and I fit comfortably in both. To this day, though, I still bathe with a cup."

Wow. Where did that come from? And why did she feel the need to fictionalize a background? Shania's real story owned plenty of drama—all the tragedy and triumph any publicist would want—but for some unfathomable reason she decided to create an alternate narrative.

Little of the outrageous tale she told was true. There were no thirteen-man crews, for instance. Her family struggled and nearly starved for most of those years; they certainly weren't supporting a crew of employees.

What else: She planted millions of trees? She worked hours from civilization? She dedicated five years of her life to that kind of work in Timmins? None of it was true.

Shania also raised another conceit in the bio. She implied that, to her, music provides a means "to experience all those feelings we need to express." That can be true, but it was clear that music, for Shania at least, was about escaping deeply felt emotions, not exploring them.

But, in an introductory bio, a person can be whoever they want to be. Shania apparently wanted to be somebody else.

"I'm a pretty emotional person," she said, a statement that likely would surprise those who knew her, and one that she would contradict in interviews after she became famous, when she was more likely to admit that she tended to be composed, tightly self-controlled, and anything but emotional.

But a record company bio isn't meant to be anything more than a superficial introduction to a record. The first time anyone in the media saw the bio came when Mercury mailed out Shania's first single, the upbeat "What Made You Say That."

To help promote the song, Mercury invested in an expensive video set on a Miami beach. In retrospect, it seemed to be an odd choice. While the steel-drum parts in "What Made You Say That" certainly gave the tune a tropical, tourist atmosphere, Shania was being touted as a citizen of the rugged Great White North. If her album cover and her publicity photos picture her in banks of snow bundled in heavy clothing and standing next to a wolf, why would the company then choose to send out a first video showing her dancing in sand on a beach?

The images greatly contradicted each other and probably confused those trying to get a handle on who this new singer was.

Nonetheless, the video for "What Made You Say That" introduced what would later become Shania's greatest marketing tool—her navel. As she sashayed around on the beach in Florida, what was to become the most famous belly button in country music history received its worldwide premiere.

The sandy beachfront setting likely was chosen because

of the songs spry steel-drum segment. Besides, the sunny setting gave Shania an excuse to shed some clothing.

Until Shania came along, the country music industry tended toward an arch uptightness as far as the images of women were concerned. As with American politics or the Republican Party, a small but aggressively vocal part of the country music audience owned conservative values. Any overt suggestion of sexuality was considered taboo—or at least it had been until the invasion of Shania and her world-class belly button.

On "What Made You Say That," Shania sashayed with a come-on glare in her eye, cavorting on the beach with a muscular, well-tanned fellow who looked like he leapt off the pages of the *International Male* clothes catalog.

In what would become an important aspect of Shania's rise to fame, the video for "What Made You Say That" seemed to attract men of power to her. The first was actor Sean Penn, the mercurial California resident who had become known as an intense actor. An unpredictable and sometimes violent public presence, Penn had gained notoriety beyond his acting ability while married to Madonna.

By the time he contacted Shania, Penn had divorced the famous Material Girl and attempted to disappear from the public eye. He concentrated for a few years on directing and screenwriting while trying to put all the public hoopla behind him. It was during that time that he let it be known that he found Shania fascinating and would be interested in directing her in a video.

Shania Twain as she wants to be seen: an elegant yet earthy outdoorswoman with more than a hint of sex appeal

If Shania looks comfortable standing atop this grand
Andalusian steed, it's because they're good friends.
Shania's favorite horse from her personal stable,
Dancer, was hauled across North America by a trainer
during the singer's 1998-99 tour so she could ride
him when she wished.

TOP Shania sits between country star Vince Gill (*right*) and MCA Nashville chairman Bruce Hinton (*left*) prior to the annual City of Hope softball match, a traditional June charity event that features country stars battling it out in friendly competition.

BOTTOM Shania helps dish out dessert to underprivileged children as part of her Kids Café program, a charity she formed to feed inner-city children. The charity is run with assistance from the Second Harvest Food Bank.

Flashing the navel that changed Nashville, Shania displays the fashion sense that moved country music into a new era where its style is hip and progressive rather than conservative and traditional.

Courtesy of Barry Hollywood/Mercury Records

Standing on an outdoor plaza atop the Nashville headquarters of Broadcast Music Inc., Shania graciously accepts several awards for her songwriting and for the radio airplay of her hit songs.

Photo by Raeanne Rubenstein

Courtesy of Allen Beaulieu/Mercury Records

On February 10, 1996, Shania drew 20,000 people to the Mall of America in Minneapolis even though she was there only to sign autographs and do a live radio interview. Above, she's seen discussing her background with a radio deejay; below, she waves to the fans who flooded every level of the spacious mall to catch a glimpse of her.

Courtesy of Allen Beaulieu/Mercury Records

Photo by Raeanne Rubenstein

In 1996, at a time when she wasn't touring, Shania gave a rare performance at the annual International Country Music Fan Fair event in Nashville. Two more years would pass before she staged a full-out concert tour.

Shania prances in the surf in Florida as video director Steven Goldmann captures the performance. The video for "What Made You Say That," though not a hit, was what first drew the attention of Robert "Mutt" Lange, Shania's future husband and record producer.

Courtesy of Cynthia Biederman/Mercury Records

Unlike many female country music stars of previous generations, Shania is completely comfortable posing for ornate glamour shots or putting on a sultry, sexy act for the camera. On the left above she strikes a famous pose, snapped by celebrated photographer John Derek, in a shot modeled after one used by Derek's wife, Bo, in the movie *10*. On the right Shania curls like a mermaid ready to be transported to the ball.

In one of the biggest concert tours of 1998, Shania took her music to stages
across North America. Though reviews were mixed, the tour finally
put to rest the rumor that Shania was a studio concoction who
couldn't entertain or carry a tune live.

Of course someone was interested. Hardly anyone had shown any interest in Shania at this point—certainly not radio programmers, anyway. The radio single for "What Made You Say That" didn't even make the Top 40; it stalled at number fifty-five on the country singles chart, which meant it never really received any significant airplay on major country stations in urban areas.

But Sean Penn liked it. That at least stood for something. Together, he and Shania created a warm, period-piece video for the song "Dance with the One That Brought You," featuring heavyset character actor Charles Durning, who it turns out, is quite a dancer. The video had a nostalgic feel and was set at an old-fashioned barn dance in a generic country setting.

As Shania's two videos were receiving mild airplay on country video stations, she was sent out by her record company on what was billed as the "Triple Play" tour. Conceived by new Mercury Nashville president Luke Lewis, the Triple Play concept was designed to introduce three new artists to radio and to fans simultaneously.

Because it can be hard to get anyone interested in a new act, Mercury thought that allowing both industry insiders and fans a chance to see three new performers at once might prove novel enough to draw crowds to shows.

But the strategy backfired: The crowds were dismal and the acts' handlers squabbled behind the scenes.

In retrospect, the idea of the tour seems questionable from the start: Why would anyone want to spend an evening watching three performers they didn't know? Usually a new act starts out by opening shows for better-known performers; that way, audiences who come to see the headliner may end up liking the warm-up act as well. For newcomers, such arrangements assure that at least someone will be in front of them when they sing.

For the Triple Play tour, there were no marquee names, so the only people in the audiences were those willing to trade away an evening for free tickets and drinks provided by the record company. Even when small audiences appeared for shows, people in the crowd were more interested in freebies and in talking business than in listening to new music.

Of the three artists sent on tour—Toby Keith, John Brannen, and Shania Twain—only one ended the tour better known than before it started. Toby Keith, a tall and broad-shouldered ex-college football star, was really the only performer on the tour with a connection to traditional country music. He wore a hat, and in a muscular baritone, he sang spirited honky tonk and romantic ballads that cut through to country audiences.

As the tour got underway, Keith also was enjoying his first hit, "Should've Been a Cowboy." His first single, it ended up spending two weeks at number-one on the country charts. Shania's "What Made You Say

That," by contrast, only reached number fifty-five before dying off.

Brannen fared even worse. A former hard rock singer giving country a try after failing to score in pop music, Brannen never got on the radio charts at all. He faded away after one album, as do many who fail to get a quick response after putting out a debut album.

For Shania, whose performances depend heavily on sharing energy with a crowd, the tour was a disaster. Without anyone to respond to her music, there was no vitality, no enthusiastic exchange.

Keith garnered most of the press and radio attention, because he had a hit on the airwaves. On occasion, someone would ask to talk to Shania, drawn by her hardscrabble story or her Canadian heritage. When that happened, she continued to elaborate on the fictional tales she'd originated for her record company bio.

"I never really decided to pursue a recording career until last year," she told one reporter. "But once I did, everything just seemed to fall into place. I know I'm going to be asked a lot about my hard-luck stories in getting a record deal. I don't have any. My hard-luck story was growing up. The music has been the easy part."

But interest in Shania was scant. For the singer, it reminded her of the days of long ago, when her parents took her around to perform for numbed drinkers who looked, but didn't dance or respond in anyway. At least at Deerhurst, she always had a good crowd. Now, here she was, singing someone else's songs and playing for empty rooms. It was not what she dreamed would happen when she put out her first album.

In fact, Shania may have joined Brannen as a record label casualty if not for another call. As with Sean Penn, the call was inspired by Shania's video, "What Made You Say That." Unlike Penn, Mary Bailey didn't recognize the name of the caller.

Speaking with a not-quite-definable accent, the caller explained that he was a record producer and songwriter. His name, he said, was Robert John Lange. People called him "Mutt," he told Bailey.

Mutt Lange was living in London at the time. Fortunately for both Shania and him, Country Music Television had invested heavily in a European satellite network. CMT, like its big-brother station the Nashville Network, was owned at the time by Gaylord Entertainment and the CBS-affiliated Westinghouse broadcasting system.

Rather than run the same video program as shown in America, CMT executives figured that Europeans tended to enjoy country music that had stronger pop and rock influences than U.S. fans did. So while Shania's video received minimal airplay in America, it gained more frequent airings in Europe.

As fate would have it, Lange enjoyed relaxing to CMT's European music. Though best known for producing rock acts like Def Leppard and AC/DC, Lange privately enjoyed country music. One day while flipping between soccer matches and CMT, he happened to catch an enchanting, dark-haired singer as she went through her paces with characteristic cool poise. He liked what he saw. Reserved by nature, he nonetheless felt compelled to contact her. He wanted to know more about her.

Though Mary Bailey had never heard of him, polite woman that she was, she listened graciously. Then she thanked him for his interest, wrote down a mailing address, and promised to send out a package. Then, with little to-do, she hung up, not realizing she had just spoken with one of the most successful record producers of the modern rock era.

After putting down the receiver, she put a black-and-white autographed photo of Shania in a manila envelope, along with a standard Mercury Records press kit and a copy of the Shania Twain CD. She put it in the mail and moved along, not giving Lange another thought.

Lange must have chuckled when he received the package. He called again, pressing Mary Bailey a bit harder this time. He would love to talk to Shania and tell her how much he enjoyed her music. That made Mary furrow her brow, but she promised to look into it for him.

Bailey contacted Shania. The singer had never heard of him, either. "I thought he was a fan who was a songwriter," she later said. So the manager contacted Luke Lewis at Mercury Records to ask about Lange. Luke responded with unfettered amazement: "Mutt Lange called asking about Shania Twain?!"

As Lewis excitedly explained, Lange had produced an incredible number of monster hits: AC/DC's "Back In

Black," "Highway to Hell," and "Shook Me All Night Long;" Def Leppard's "Pour Some Sugar on Me;" Billy Ocean's "Get Outta My Dreams, Get Into My Car;" Bryan Adams' "Everything I Do (I Do For You);" and many, many more.

"What did he say?" Lewis asked. Mary explained that this Mutt guy had seen a video of Shania's, the beach-front clip for "What Made You Say That." By the end, Mary reiterated that Lange was interested in talking or meeting with Shania. "Should she put them in touch?" Mary asked Luke, somewhat incredulously. The record executive retorted, "Yes, by all means."

When Shania first found out about Lange's successful track record, she at first "pretended I always knew," she said. "It turned out I loved everything he ever did. I just didn't know it was him."

Bailey set up the first phone conversation, having Shania call the producer. As Shania has often said, they hit it off immediately. They began holding regular conversations, often talking for astounding lengths of time.

"Every conversation we had was a good three hours long," Shania told *USA Today* in 1995.

Lange would listen as Shania played her own songs on the guitar, over the phone. Shania would rest the telephone receiver on her pillow, let a leg dangle from the mattress, and cradle an acoustic guitar in her lap. Then she'd sing the songs she'd written. The same songs Norro Wilson and Harold Shedd didn't want her to record.

She sang a melodic, upbeat song called "Any Man of Mine." Then she nervously picked up the phone. Lange, one of the world's most successful record crafters, told her he loved it. He wanted to hear more. She sang a gentle, melodic ballad called "Home Ain't Where the Heart Is (Anymore)." He loved it, too.

She had originality, he told her. Why hadn't she recorded her own songs? she asked. Shania wondered the same thing, she excitedly told him.

"What's wrong with those people?!" Mutt would say. They'd laugh, but Mutt would assure his new friend that he meant it. Those songs are good, he would tell her. They're fresh, they're different, and they have great potential. They just needed to be put with the right musical support.

He praised her voice, too, even though he heard it only through the transmission of fiber cable. "The way you're singing right now," he told her after a couple of songs, "even though it's over the phone, that's the voice I've heard bits and pieces of in the album that I have. That's how you should be sounding all the time. If you're doing your own stuff, you'll be able to get that."

The frequency of their phone conversations started to increase. Lange had been putting the finishing touches on a Bryan Adams album, and he occasionally spoke to Adams about this woman in Nashville.

Lange and Adams had collaborated on several albums, and along the way became good friends. Adams liked

Nashville, he told Lange. So the producer made a suggestion: Want to go there with me?

Shania had told Lange that she planned to spend a
week in Nashville in June of 1993 for the annual International Country Music Fan Fair convention. A one-of-
a-kind event, Fan Fair draws 25,000 rabid country music
fans to Nashville each summer for a marathon week of
music, fan-club parties, and autograph sessions.

Shania knew that her career hung in the wind. Mercury would decide whether she should make a second
album or not, and so far she had not gained any firm
commitment from the company.

Indeed, the only time she heard any enthusiasm from
Mercury Records came after Mutt Lange had entered
the picture. After that, most of her conversations with
top-ranking Mercury executives concerned Lange:
Might he be interested in producing her next album? For
the first time, Mercury was talking as if a next record was
expected to happen.

So, when Lange suggested he might travel to Nashville for Fan Fair to meet her, Shania was thrilled. Was it
for romantic reasons? Was it because they had begun to
collaborate on a couple of song ideas? Was it because she
saw him as a potential producer?

In truth, it may have been all three. They'd been writing songs together by Federal Express at this point. Both
of them had hinted at the idea of working together as
producer and artist. And, even though Shania had yet to
mention it to anyone, she felt butterflies of excitement

pass through her when she thought of actually meeting this friendly mystery man in person.

Adams agreed to travel with Lange to Fan Fair. Backstage at the Mercury Records show, they stood off to the side, Lange combing the crowd with his eyes as Adams greeted well-wishers who recognized him. The shaggy-haired Mutt eyed Shania before she saw him. She was surrounded by Mercury Records personnel as she walked through the backstage area, heading towards a tent where Lange stood, watching and waiting.

When she saw him, after someone pointed in his direction, she ran up to him and leapt into his arms, as if greeting a longlost friend or lover.

When talking about their first face-to-face meeting, Shania has said that their hug was intense and long-lasting. "When I first saw him, I gave him a big, big hug," Shania noted. "I'm not a huggy person, but I was really drawn to him."

Yes, she would say later, she felt sparks—a fireworks display's worth.

Mutt had told her that he traveled to Nashville for several reasons: He wanted to meet her, of course; he wanted to discuss the production possibilities with her and Mercury Records; he wanted to work on songs; and he wanted to see her perform. What he didn't tell her, but what he wanted most of all, was to look into her eyes and see if it felt as electric in person as it did when they spoke by phone. It did.

He did, however, get to talk to executives from Mercury Records. That week, they all agreed that he would be their first choice for a producer. Mercury Records and Luke Lewis had only one concern: money. Lange was one of the most expensive producers in the business, and his recording budgets were three-to-five times as much as normal country recording expenditures.

Lange was the one who spoke up. Don't worry about it, he said. He understood the situation. It could be worked out, he said.

He also spent some time writing with her, though most of those hours were spent laughing and telling stories. He also got to see her perform, and he told her that he loved the ebullient spirit she displayed. She worked hard to entertain the conservative crowd, he said, and he was glad to see how they responded.

However, she drew one of the smallest crowds of the week. In truth, few in the crowd recognized her name or her songs. The best any of her singles had done at that point was reach number fifty-five on the country music charts. She performed well, considering the tough circumstances, but there was nothing about the crowd response to engender any excitement. But Lange told her she was great.

If Shania's spirit was flagging, Lange at least seemed undeterred by her lack of success. He clearly saw something in her ability that Norro Wilson and Harold Shedd had overlooked. Ignored both by radio programmers and country music buyers, Shania's debut album offered little encouragement to anyone, it seems, except Lange.

At the time, it wouldn't have been unusual for Shania to lose her record deal. But suddenly Mercury Records seemed more interested in her than ever. Lange's sudden presence in her camp changed everything for her. Because of him, and him alone, Shania switched from being a disappointment to carrying high hopes.

As recording time drew near, it became apparent that Lange was the only person who wanted to produce Shania's next record. Mercury loved the idea, too, but grew nervous again as it came time to draw up the contracts.

Country record budgets run much smaller than those for the high-end rock artists with whom Mutt usually collaborated. His involvement in her career certainly raised hopes, but it by no means guaranteed anything. Mutt had never enjoyed any success in country music or on country radio. Moreover, he had a reputation for extravagant spending in the studio, spending months and months making a record and running up costs of a half million or more—an unheard of sum for a country album.

Eventually, he officially proposed the idea: He'd like to produce Shania's next album, he told Luke Lewis. But Lange, being the knowledgeable record man, cushioned his offer: He'd gladly absorb a majority of the upfront costs of making the record if Mercury agreed to give him a larger-than-usual cut of the proceeds.

Luke Lewis flipped with joy at the idea. "Mutt bore the risks as much as we did," Lewis says.

It was still a huge gamble for everyone. There was little excitement among anyone outside of Mercury for the next Shania Twain album, no matter who was producing. If Mutt's experiment failed, it would dig only a deeper grave for Shania. But that would be true no matter who produced it. Why not take such a gamble?

Chapter Five

The Woman in Her

WHEN SHANIA PUT OUT HER FIRST ALBUM, COUN-try music was enjoying its greatest success ever. Two years earlier, Garth Brooks had become the first country music artist ever to have a new album debut at number one on both the country and the pop charts. Country albums only rarely had led all album sales. Kenny Rogers had done it, as had Glen Campbell. But that was about it.

Now all of a sudden, country albums proliferated on the pop charts, which track all record sales, regardless of genre. Artists like Alan Jackson, Reba McEntire,

George Strait, Randy Travis, Clint Black, and Trisha Yearwood were regularly enjoying records that climbed into the Top 40 record sellers—with many of them spending time in the top ten as well.

Country record sales had been climbing steadily since the mid-1980s when Randy Travis, the Judds, Dwight Yoakam, Reba McEntire, and George Strait led a youthful surge in interest in country music. But the steady growth country music experienced suddenly skyrocketed when Brooks released a couple of monster back-to-back hits, the ballad "The Dance," and a sly party tune, "Friends in Low Places."

At that point, Brooks' sales shot through the stratosphere. From 1990 to the end of the 1993, he sold more than thirty million albums. In a six-hour period in Dallas in 1993, he sold 195,000 tickets to three consecutive concerts. With Brooks in the engine room, a long train of country music stars started counting their sales by the millions for the first time in the history of the music.

Americans had always listened to country music. They just never purchased it in big numbers. But by 1993, forty-two percent of the U.S. radio audience was tuning into country music on a regular basis. Moreover, instead of accounting for about nine percent of the annual music sales, country music doubled its market share in less than a decade. By 1993, it grabbed about eighteen-to-nineteen percent of all record sales. The following year, country music topped two billion dollars in revenue. For Nashville, the gold rush was in full swing.

Also by 1993, country music had begun introducing new performers at an unprecedented rate. Many of them broke through immediately, selling a million records after only a few hits. It was a heady time to be involved in country music, and every company padded its roster, hoping to cash in as lucratively as possible on the new interest in country music.

Shania was introduced at the peak of the growth, and she was among the few not to reap at least some response. But her first album disappeared without raising a trifle of dust on the country landscape.

But, unlike most who fail to gain a following on a debut album, Shania was more excited than ever. Ignoring her failure, she started focusing on her second album as if it was her true premiere. It would be the first time that she would be allowed to fill an album with her own material. To her, that fact proved incredibly stimulating, both creatively and personally.

Shania didn't care what was happening in country music. She loved the business aspects of a musical career, and she quietly plotted on her own. But she didn't respond to what others were doing. She had her own ideas now, and she wanted to pursue them without paying attention to what other artists created.

To start work on her second album, Shania and Lange began by scheduling writing time together. Lange suggested they make a vacation of it, suggesting the two of them jump on a Concorde aircraft and whisk away to London.

"The Concorde?" Shania asked, incredulous. She wasn't aware of the existence of the high-speed, transatlantic air carrier.

"You've never heard of the Concorde?" Lange asked back, laughing. No, she said. So he explained about the luxury aircraft, along with its amenities and excessive speeds.

The two booked a flight, then disappeared for days into Lange's expensive, extremely private home. Looking back later, Shania says it wasn't an immediate love affair, no matter how it may look to people.

"We ended up writing half the album, mind you, before we even became romantically involved," she said.

From the start, Lange planned on recording nothing but Shania's own songs. The effect on Shania was both exhilarating and incredibly liberating. To gain that kind of support from a producer with his reputation gave her a confidence she had never experienced before. What could be more romantic to the singer-songwriter, who had endured so much to get where she was, than to get this level of encouragement, this level of belief in her ability to write a song?

Shania grew up near a gold mine, but no amount of gold would have equaled how much Lange's attention meant to her.

No wonder they fell in love. By the time they emerged from their songwriting retreat, they were locked together in both heart and artistry. Shania's songs owned a point of view, a peculiar yet fresh way with words, and what she wanted was someone to help her put her ideas to up-beat melodies and energized tempos. Lange was a master at creating a particular kind of power-melody, building arrangements so that songs hammered a theme into a lis-tener's mind with all the insinuating obviousness of a Sousa march.

"It was definitely a force that brought us together," Shania has said. "Something drove him (to contact me), and I'm not sure if even he knew what it was. It was def-initely a force."

Some considered it an odd match. Lange is sixteen years older than Shania, and unlike the singer, he's obses-sive about his privacy—not the kind of profile that leads a man to become smitten with an entertainer whose en-tire life becomes public property.

Shania is driven, Lange is laid-back. Shania is in-tensely particular about her looks, from her clothes to her hair to her makeup; Lange keeps his hair shaggy and un-kempt, preferring the post-hippie look of colorful shirts and slip-on shoes.

Shania loves the camera; Lange goes to great lengths to keep himself out of photographs and out of the press. Musicians who've worked with him say he'll even ask the players not to include him in personal photos of the ses-sions; during the making of Shania's third album, *Come on Over*, instrumentalists were required to sign privacy agreements declaring that they would not divulge any in-formation about what transpired. One musician caught taking photos was addressed directly and in no uncertain terms by Lange. He stopped short of asking for the film from the camera, but he made it clear he never wanted to see those photos printed anywhere.

Shania strikes people as cold and removed; Lange is considered amiable and forthcoming. He's unusually casual for a rock record producer, especially considering the nearly pathological way he fine-tunes his recordings. He's open and generous with his time with musicians and collaborators; he invites ideas and truly listens to what those contributing to the album have to say. He has his own strong ideas, of course, and because of his dedication to layering tracks and to creating his muscular melodies, he's developed a trademark sound over the years.

The couple did have something in common, though. Lange also grew up around gold mines—his father worked as a blue-collar miner, crawling deep into the South African earth to dig out gold and asbestos for corporations.

Once they met, they became constant conspirators. The schedules kept them seeing each other every day, but they never let a twenty-four hour period pass without a long phone conversation.

The speed of their bonding shocked those who knew Shania. "She's very quiet, very reserved, and very cautious about who she lets in," Mary Bailey said of her longtime friend and client.

She wasn't cautious when it came to Lange. On Dec.

28, 1993—barely six months after the two met at Fan
Fair—they snuck off and privately married.

"He's given me the confidence to be who I am," Shania
said at the time. "He really is Mr. Wonderful."

Everyone close to Shania, from old friends to her siblings, thought it happened far too fast. What made it
stranger to them is that Shania had not displayed a pas-
sionate interest in a man before meeting Lange.

It was always one of the quirks of her character that
her family and friends discussed: Would Shania ever
truly fall in love? She'd have the occasional boyfriend,
but relationships always fell by the wayside in her pur-
suit of a career. She didn't talk about men. She talked obsessively about her career, about clothes, and how she
looked. She didn't talk about guys, or dating, or going
out and having fun.

Shania admitted as much herself. Men, relationships,
and sex—none of that ever drew much interest from her.
"The truth is," she once said of herself, "I'm distracted by
very little besides music. When it really gets down to it,
for instance, I am not a sexual person. My mind isn't
there. I mean, I'm very satisfied, and I'm not hard to sat-
isfy. But I'm not one of those people who just always has
this desire. I don't think like that. Never did. Always had
total control of my sexual habits."

That trait translates as well to how she shares affection
with others. "I'm very conservative, really," she said. "I'm
not that physical. I mean, I am with Mutt, of course, and

with my dog. But beyond that, not even with my family. I'm just not one of these hug-everybody people. I'm better now than I was. Used to be, I didn't even want my mother to hug me. I used to hate it."

Once she connected with Lange, Shania suddenly seemed more removed than ever to her loved ones. They were concerned about the decisions she was making and the distance she was putting between herself and her past.

CONSIDERING HER DIFFICULT UPBRINGING AND the tragic ending of her parents, some might expect Shania to write dark, angst-ridden songs. Obviously, pop music is filled with young songwriters who pour their most desperate and painful emotions into songs.

But Shania never turned to music for that kind of catharsis; she grew up in the late '70s and early '80s, but she wasn't drawn to the music of that era. She didn't find anything worthwhile in the physical release of punk rock, the emotional territory of urban singer-songwriters, or the social commentary of Bruce Springsteen and John Mellencamp.

Instead, Shania looked to music for escape, for entertainment that took her away from her troubles rather than helping her confront them. That kind of escapism is what she wanted to provide others. She wrote about inner strength, self-dignity, sexual teasing, and having fun. With Lange's help, she put her songs to cheery, beat-happy melodies that emphasized energy, spontaneity, and fun.

She once explained how she came up with many of her songs: "Mutt will be in the living room watching the game on TV, and I'll be cooking dinner," she said, even though her figure doesn't suggest she spends much time around a stove or a refrigerator.

Still, she says, "I'll come up with an idea for a song in the kitchen, then bring it in and tell him about it. That's a pretty typical scenario."

Having her husband support her writing meant so much to her; it freed her to explore her creativity.

"Writing's like coloring to me," she says. "Kids like to color. They don't need to have a reason to color; they just like it. Why do they use orange instead of pink, or green instead of blue? I don't know, they don't know—they just do. They have no inhibitions. They are totally open to be creative. That's how I feel about songwriting. It's a chance to just create without inhibitions."

As for the famed rock producer's move into country music, Shania said it was a transition Lange had wanted to do for a long time. "Tanya Tucker and Tammy Wynette are his two favorite female singers in the world," she said of her husband. "The steel guitar is his favorite instrument."

If Shania had a basic theme, it was that women in the '90s could have it their way—as long as they were strong, outspoken, and willing to stand up for themselves. In her songs, women will not accept men who cheat or treat them poorly; they even expect men to know better than to joke about bad hair days. As she sang in "Any Man of Mine," her first major hit, it was OK if she showed up late. It wasn't OK if he kept her waiting, however.

As simple as the music seems on the surface, Lange added complex sounds that added depth and resonance to his wife's playful, straightforward lyrics. Because of Lange's studio obsessiveness, Shania's second album took next to forever to complete.

Lange painstakingly pieced together the songs, four bars and eight bars at a time. He accentuated each melodic hook and added sonic bombast to each big beat, stacking fiddles so that it sounded like an orchestra bearing down on a simple chorus.

He enlivened the songs with flourishes of Cajun accordion and Motown-like rhythmic bounce. He leavened on the steel guitars and fiddles—this was unmistakably a country music record, but nothing like any country music album previously recorded. That was clear in arena-like rock drums, the elaborate guitar solos, and the shifting rhythms that always kept the energy high.

Lange didn't work alone or without her input, Shania would say time and again. It was a collaboration, not a case of mastermind and puppet.

"It's true that Mutt thinks more along the lines of production than I do," she said. "When we're writing a song, we might throw ideas out. I might say, 'This would be great with a fiddle.' Or he will say, 'This is the type of guitar sound we should go for on this song.' We'll talk through stuff like that during the songwriting process, but it isn't until you get in the studio that you start experimenting with it."

Not only did he help his wife with her songs; he also set an environment that allowed her to get the best out of her voice.

"You don't always know what your best points are and what your weak points are," Shania said after the album was issued. "It's hard for a singer to be objective about herself. A good producer knows what those elements are."

Obviously, she was very happy with the result and with how it was received. "His production introduced country music to a new sound," she said. "It contributed greatly to the success of the record. In a way, everyone has done everything that can be done, so people reinvent things. But Mutt has his own thing that he puts in everything he does. There was room for something fresh in country. And the combination between the two of us is new."

In the end, the couple spent more than a year making the album. By the time they finished, Shania was his wife. Mercury Records has said that Lange spent $500,000 creating the album. Truth is, had he been billing them by the hour at his usual rate, it would have been much, much more than that.

Once the album became a hit, plenty of people suggested that Shania was little more than a voice amid Lange's magic, a puppet he maneuvered into playing a role in a larger production.

Shania saw it differently, of course. To her, Lange allowed her to express herself as a writer as well as a singer, giving her a soundstage on which she could be herself.

"I've been a singer-songwriter all of my life," she told journalist Calvin Gilbert. "On my first album, I was introduced as only a singer and not as a songwriter. It was sort of like only half of me got introduced."

In her first interviews after making her second album, *The Woman in Me,* Shania fully shared credit for what she and her husband had concocted. "Creatively, romantically, it's a wonderful, wonderful marriage," she said. "My husband Mutt is the producer of my dreams and the love of my life. They are two separate entities, but at the same time what more can any girl ask for?"

Later, however, she changed her angle, no doubt to battle those who said she had little input into her own recording.

"The reality is, it's all me," she said in her defense. "The songs are as country and as rock and pop as they are because that's what I am. I pick everything I wear, everything I do, every move I make. I am directing myself artistically, period; no ifs, ands, or buts about it."

Still, *The Woman in Me* sounded vastly different than anything she'd ever done on her own. To Shania, though, it was because she was showing her true self for the first time.

"The songs definitely show more attitude," she said. "And that attitude is mine."

Moreover, *The Woman in Me* easily ranked as the most expensive country music album ever made—a highly unusual move for someone whose first album bombed.

Luke Lewis, the head of Mercury Nashville, is among those to openly credit the importance of Lange's role. "You can't take away [Mutt's] contribution to the album," Lewis told writer Laurence Leamer.

Later, during the BMI celebration for Shania prior to her first Nashville concert, Lewis said, "[Lange] might be the best record producer of the century. When music historians look back on this era, his name will stand above the others for all the great music he's made. He's under-recognized now, but his accomplishments will speak for themselves. They do now, and they'll speak even louder for him in the future."

Indeed, Lange is the ultimate sonic architect. His method of working completely subverts the conception people have of a singer performing in a studio surrounded by musicians playing their instruments live and all together. Instead, a producer like Lange assembles each note with painstaking care, taking what musicians have played and tweaking it, moving it around, and eventually coming up with a sound no one ever could create without sonic effects.

Lange spent a year in the studio constructing and reconstructing each song on *The Woman in Me* with obsessive attention to detail. He'd record a vocal, then layer them on top of each other to create an unusual and exhilarating vocal effect. He likes to give vocal parts the power of a choir, making each note resonate with a strength unreachable by a single voice. It's as artificial as it can be, but the point is to create something that sounds spontaneous; that's one of the reasons Shania adds so many spoken asides to her songs. It makes the song sound live and off-the-cuff.

This method of creating music has its detractors. There are those who criticize the deceit involved, and there are those who say that the technique removes the human element from the music. But it works because it sells.

SHANIA AND LANGE SPARED NO EXPENSE IN CRE-ating a new image that would fit her new music. Shania employed a photographer and filmmaker, John Derek, who was known for his ideas of beauty and glamour. The husband of actress and model Bo Derek, and the ex-lover of such famed females as Jane Fonda and Brigette Bardot, Derek created idealized visions of women.

As with Lange, Derek worked in a dictatorial style, imposing his sense of style upon his subject. But Twain wanted to show the world an image that was both glamorous and earthy, and she loved Derek's work.

However, Derek didn't necessarily love Shania. At least he wasn't enamored with her looks.

To explain, Shania recalled her first meeting with the

photographer. "He sees me, and I'm like a monster to him. He says, 'Somebody give me a knife! I've got to cut that nose off,'" she said, laughing when retelling the story. But, as she was quick to point out, "It wasn't funny at the time."

Remember, this was before she was a star, before anyone knew she would be famous, before young girls and boys hung posters of her in their bedrooms. At the time, Derek's comments were just another devastating blow that she overcame.

It says something about Shania's personal makeup that, despite Derek's original assessment of her, they nonetheless were able to work together. They even became friends, staying in touch long after the photos were finished. In fact, when John Derek died in the summer of 1998, Shania was one of the first people Bo Derek called to share the difficult news.

Moreover, as another sign of her steely and determined nature, Shania went ahead and worked through rehearsal the evening she got the news, despite the shock and pain she felt for her deceased friend and the grieving widow.

"You know, it was kind of a drag," she told *Rolling Stone* when recounting her finding out about her friend's death.

Still, the fact that she went ahead with the rehearsal said a lot about her. "I didn't want anybody to see me, 'cause I hate that affecting me," she said. But she caught herself, realizing that what she said could be translated as being cold. "Of course, it has to affect me. You don't want to say, 'I'm not bummed out,' or 'I have to forget that I'm bummed out.' It was just a terrible thing. It was a very sudden thing . . . So now Bo's alone. It keeps freaking me out a bit."

WITH THE RELEASE OF THE ALBUM, IT WAS OBVIous that Shania was more confident in who she was and where she had come from. She no longer tried to suggest that music was something she accidentally entered.

Instead, this time her record company bio told a different story. She must have figured that no one paid attention to the first one anyway.

"I pretty much missed my childhood," she said at the beginning of the bio. "I've always been focused. My career has always been very consuming. It probably consumes me less now than it did as a child. Music was all I ever did."

In analyzing the songs on the album, Shania made a wise prediction that would prove quite intuitive. Talking about the song "Any Man of Mine," she said, "I think it could be the impact song of this album. It is an excellent combination of the two of us. It's got everything that he's known for as a producer and a writer, yet it's so me it's not funny. The title cut is another good example of a collaboration of our two backgrounds. It really is the two of us right down the middle."

When the album came out, it didn't exactly find critics lining up to heap praise upon it. In *Entertainment Weekly*, veteran country music reviewer Alanna Nash wrote, "What do you get when you pair a former Canadian resort singer with a Karen Carpenter fixation and an over-the-top pop producer who thinks it would be fun to work in country? One of the worst records of the decade." She gave it a grade of F, a rarity for the weekly magazine.

Others heard it differently, however. Tom Roland of *The Tennessean*, Nashville's daily newspaper, wrote "This is an absolutely stunning album. A lot of country artists have melded the idiom with rock 'n' roll in a way that's beome entirely predictable, but not Twain. Working with husband/producer Robert John "Mutt" Lange, they wrote the entire project and created an album that blends elements from two styles without watering down either one."

David Ross, editor of a Nashville trade magazine, *Music Row*, also didn't agree with those critics who heard the album as overly studied and fussed over. Instead, he described it as "beautifully cool because it's so unique. I think that's what the format is crying out for."

Most of the album featured upbeat, playful songs, including the initial hits "Whose Bed Have Your Boots Been Under" and "Any Man of Mine."

But there were serious moments, too. "God Bless the

Child" was a lullabye inspired by her parents' death that Shania had written many years earlier.

"My thoughts often get expressed musically," she said. "That song was about how I felt sorry for myself. It was symbolic of what I was going through. My parents were kidnapped from me and I was left standing there. For years, I would sing this lullaby to soothe me."

Lange, who considers the ballad one of his favorite of his wife's songs, insisted that she sing it a cappella on the album. "I felt kind of weird about it, kind of like somebody reading my diary," she says of the song. "But now I almost don't relate to it anymore because there are real suffering children out there."

As for the album's variety, Shania said that was simply a representation of her broad tastes in music. She repeatedly pointed out that Timmins only had one hometown radio station when she was young, and "it played every kind of music mixed together."

She considered herself lucky to have enjoyed that kind of experience so young. "I was able to listen to all the best music in all the genres," she said. "That's the way I've always seen music. I love all kind of music."

Besides, she adds, variety suits her personality as well. "I get bored very quickly and have to move on a lot," Shania explained. "That's part of being a woman, I guess—especially a growing one. You're going to continue to see that kind of variety from me."

Besides, she emphasized, this album truly represents

all aspects of her character, both artistically and personally. That wasn't true on her first album, she noted.

"Being yourself is what is going to make you unique," she says. "That is the best advice I can give anyone."

As for the expensive, careful production, she suggested country music was behind the times if it didn't spend as much money as she did when making records.

"Listen," she told writer James Hunter, "the audience has sophisticated ears. The audience that watches any kind of television and listens to any kind of audio gets the top quality just through ads. Hey, they have to be able to go from a Coke ad or a Janet Jackson record to my record and not notice the difference in quality. There's no reason we shouldn't be at that level. That's absolutely been my goal from the beginning."

That worldly sense of sound and marketing began to saturate Shania's interviews. Like a lot of modern artists, she didn't perceive artifice in music as a bad thing. Everyone knew that making music was a business, and that openly positioning oneself in the marketplace was being smart, not manipulative. She figured that was what stars do. What was authenticity or honesty in packaging other than just another calculated strategy?

"Our job in country music right now as artists has to be to keep those listeners that would just as soon turn over to a light rock or adult contemporary station," she said. "We have to give those people what they want to hear in order to keep them there. They love to hear the rock influence, the blues influence, all the influences that are also considered very American. We've got a R&B genre, a light R&B, '70s rock stations, and AC stations that we could put out of business if we were. clever enough to keep that audience."

TO INITIATE THE INTRODUCTION OF THE NEW Shania, Mercury Records released a video for "Whose Bed Have Your Boots Been Under." Directed by John Derek, the video was a sumptuous, playful bit of soft erotica. To try and build momentum for Shania, the video was sent to the Country Music Television cable channel before the single was given to radio stations.

Initially however, CMT barely played it, to the great consternation of Mercury Records. The panel of CMT employees who reviewed new video submissions consisted almost wholly of women, and Luke Lewis surmised that perhaps the women felt uncomfortable watching such an attractive, uninhibited woman gyrate around in sexy, navel-baring attire.

"I think their official response was that the video was redundant and boring," Lewis later reflected. "We felt that they felt it was a little too sexy and that's why they didn't want to play it much."

Later, CMT would take credit for helping launch Shania's career, a boast that upset the staff of Mercury

Records, which knew better. "They deserve absolutely no credit for the success," Lewis said.

Shania also reacted with disbelief when told her video was too sexy. To her, baring her navel is hardly what she would call overt or risqué. "I know people think, 'Well, she's not very inhibited, she bares her midriff.' I'm like, 'Well, big deal, I bear my midriff. That's not really sexual.' "

Of course, Shania being who she is, it's curious to those who know her that she's able to come across as so flirtatious and sexually suggestive on camera. In person, she's not like that at all. As liberated as she seems, especially in her choice of clothing, she's actually conservative to the point of uptightness in real life.

"I will only wear a bathing suit with a wrap, unless I'm really being daring," she told *Rolling Stone*. "Oh, sometimes I get free-spirited enough to actually say, 'I don't give a shit!' But it doesn't happen often. Like, even if I was the only person on the beach that wasn't topless, I would not take my bathing suit top off. My husband would go, 'Why not? Every other woman on this beach is topless.' But I couldn't. It's just the way I am."

Though "Whose Bed Have Your Boots Been Under" went on to become a country radio staple through 1996 and 1997, radio programmers didn't eagerly embrace it at first, either. It didn't crack the all-important Top 10 of the country music charts, hitting a roadblock at number 11.

The subject matter—a lighthearted song about a woman confronting a cheating man—put off some radio programmers. Others thought the theme of a woman putting a man down hurt her with the conservative men who decide what gets played on the airwaves.

"A lot of men sing the cheating songs as uptempo," Shania told *USA Today*. "They can make fun of cheating songs and get away with it, while women usually sing those types of songs as ballads."

Still, Shania was thrilled with its success; it was her first country music hit. "I'm proud of that one because the title and the hook seem to be getting everybody's attention," she said. "It's really cool to be able to come up with a hook that someone like Mutt believes in."

Mercury quickly followed with "Any Man of Mine," a song that many journalists and radio personnel suggested had a chorus that sounded suspiciously close to the one used on Def Leppard's massive rock hit, "Pour Some Sugar on Me," which Lange had produced.

"It has a rock edge, for sure," Shania said of "Any Man of Mine." "But it's also undeniably country. It was just a refreshing way to present country music, so the fans embrace that, the whole playfulness of it. I don't know. I guess it's just my own way of doing country. It wasn't something that was overly planned. But I do think country music was ready for something like it."

Again, another playfully sexy video accompanied the release of the single. Again, the single gained great support from many urban stations. Still, there were stations that held back. It seemed as if the single's momentum would die before it climbed into the Top 10. Everyone involved began to worry that their potential hit album wouldn't get enough support from radio to reach the audience it needed to fulfill its potential.

Since then, rumors have suggested that Lange went to work behind the scenes to provide some emergency support for the album. A conventional, if somewhat underhanded, way of manipulating radio activity would be to pour money into independent promotion companies, who would then concentrate more effort and resources into persuading the executives who select which songs get programmed to give more air time to "Any Man of Mine."

At the same time, Lange could buy large blocks of advertising time on key radio stations, hoping to pressure radio programmers into keeping the song in heavy rotation. Such pressure shouldn't influence what songs get played, programmers often say, but it undoubtedly does. Programmers and station managers are under great pressure to increase revenues, and if playing a single would ensure that the advertising dollars would keep rolling in, then the station is likely to stick with the song and to play it more frequently.

In Nashville, many industry insiders insist that Lange even took another, extraordinary step to save "Any Man of Mine" and propel the accompanying *The Woman in Me* album into moving up the charts. What some insiders attest occurred was that Lange, who knew how record companies and record charts work, arranged to buy a huge number of albums, storing them in a warehouse.

The enormous jump in album sales affected the life of the single, since radio programmers monitor the album sales charts to determine how much fans like the music being played.

To radio stations, when records begin to sell in large numbers, it means that fans like it enough not only to listen to it on the radio but to buy it for personal play. It's a great indicator of what the people like to hear, and radio will often respond to a leap in sales by playing the song more often, figuring that it's become a favorite of their listeners.

Whatever happened, "Any Man of Mine" was saved just as it was about to die. Suddenly, it seemed, stations began to play it more rather than less. Just as suddenly, momentum began to tumble in Shania's favor. CMT began airing the videos more frequently; radio stations began playing both "Any Man of Mine" and "Whose Bed Have Your Boots Been Under" more often; and, indeed, people did respond by buying the album.

As the summer of 1995 burned on, Shania became as hot as a July day in the South. Shania began compiling sales numbers usually reserved for such top country acts as Garth Brooks, Alan Jackson, Tim McGraw, and George Strait. Then at some point, albums started flying out of stores in unprecedented numbers.

"What's overwhelming is that once it started happening, it happened so rapidly," Shania said in the middle of the sales explosion. "My head is spinning."

In truth, country music had witnessed such a phenomenon before, but only once. When Garth Brooks released his *No Fences* album in 1990, sales took off at a level the Nashville music industry had never experienced.

In the mid-1980s, sales of one million copies of an album were considered remarkable and somewhat rare. Garth Brooks rewrote the rule book; his *No Fences* album sold five million copies in a matter of months. By 1991, when he released his *Ropin' the Wind* album, advance orders stood at an astonishing four million. Between 1989 and 1992, he sold 30 million albums—becoming the hottest-selling recording act of all-time.

By 1995, however, Garth Brooks could no longer expect each album to quickly sell five million copies. That summer, for the first time in the '90s, he was usurped as country music's biggest-selling artist. That title now belonged to Shania Twain.

"I think when *The Woman in Me* came out, country was so much calmer," she told *Country Song Roundup*. "But years ago, country had a lot of extremes. When I was a kid, country was more extreme than it is now. Those are all my influences—things like Johnny Paycheck's 'Take That Job and Shove It.' I think that if somebody wrote that and did that today, that would stick out. I think the extremes, the edges, got rounded off for awhile. My influences are more from when I was younger, and people were definitely more in your face in country music then, lyrically and musically and everything. It was much rawer then. It got smooth. So when *The Woman in Me* came out, it seemed like I was maybe edgier than I really was, and a lot of fans who were there were really familiar with country music years ago, and it was an edge that wasn't new to them. I think people underestimate the fans is more my point."

SHANIA'S MUSIC DIDN'T JUST CARRY MORE OF AN edge; it also had a distinct personality, something the hits of country music didn't always own in the '90s.

"It is about personality," she said. "It's about character and the profile of a person's creativity. You have to be different. If you allow somebody to be as artistic I was, if you give them that much freedom—or if you take the freedom, which is kinda what I did—then all of a sudden you get something original."

By the time Fan Fair rolled around again in June of 1995, the indications of the enormity of Shania's success began to bloom. It was becoming obvious that country music had another record-breaker on its hands.

The last time Shania appeared at Fan Fair, she received polite attention from a handful of those attending the event. In 1995, however, she was one of the hottest attractions.

During a three-song performance in the middle of the week, the crowd went berserk. Attentive but not particularly rowdy, the conservative Fan Fair crowd tended to prefer established stars and older veterans. They come to see favorites more than discover new stars.

But Twain's energetic show lifted the crowd. Twisting on her heels, smiling and playfully rousing the crowd as she performed her recent radio hits, Shania sparkled on-stage. It was a sign of times to come, and perhaps the best preview she was to give of what she was capable of doing when given the chance to perform her own music.

David Ross, the editor of *Music Row*, a Nashville-based trade magazine, was among those in the crowd at Shania's Fan Fair performance that year.

"She really kind of made friends with the women, and since the women are the ones that buy the most (albums), it was a terribly intelligent way to handle things," Ross said. "And, in her case, she's got the men's interest anyway."

However, it wouldn't be until much later that the Fan Fair attendees realized how special and rare their glimpse of Shania on stage would be.

For the rest of the event, Shania proved to be a real workhorse. She committed herself to meeting as many fans as possible during the unusual event. Lines at her autograph booth often stretched throughout the building, and fans began lining up for an autograph from her hours before she was scheduled to arrive.

Shania worked her autograph booth for two-to-four hours a day, an amazing and rare effort to greet her new fans. Most stars dedicate a couple of hours in the early morning or late afternoon. Twain expended a great amount of time, and she devoted herself to each day with vibrancy and focus. Other stars cut off their lines once their time expired; no matter how long someone might have been waiting, they were out of luck if they didn't get past the spot where a star's handlers cut off a line.

Shania didn't treat her fans that way. Within a few months, she would be competing with Garth Brooks as the biggest country star of the decade. But at this time she stayed until everyone in line got an autograph.

Still, Shania's matter of factness already was being translated by some fans as removed, distant, even calculating. Writer Laurence Leamer described her as "a mechanical doll, flashing a smile for (the fan's) cameras, and then looking to the next person in line."

But those who watched her at length that year tell a different story. Shania connected with nearly every one of the thousands of people who came through her line that year. She established contact, warmly, and listened to their stories, responding with genuine interest.

"She was the model country star, what you think they're supposed to be like," said an industry worker who watched her one afternoon. She stepped out from behind the wooden structure, removing the protective barrier and allowing fans closer, more personal contact. These were hard-working people, and she related to them. They weren't any different than those who would crowd into the Hotel Mattagami in Timmins to see her.

To Shania, it was a moment she savored. She'd longed for contact with fans. She wasn't touring, wasn't performing, for a reason that would later be revealed. But that didn't mean she didn't want to hear the gratifying words of her fans and see their eyes light up as they got close to her.

Those who saw her that day say that Shania's problem wasn't relating with regular folk; instead, she seemed to have trouble dealing with music industry workers more. She could talk to working people; she trusted them and knew them. She couldn't necessarily warm up to those in the record industry, however. They wanted something from her, and she expected something from them. Part of her reputation as being cold comes from those she works with most closely. It doesn't come from the fans she's been in close contact with.

Most remarkably, those she gave the most to were the disabled fans, who were given a special time so they could get their autographs without the hassles of the hot afternoon crowds. For each disabled fan who came to her booth that day, Shania stood in front of her signing table, not behind it. She greeted each person warmly, often crouching over to share eye-level contact, and spoke at length with every one of the fans, many of whom were bound to wheelchairs.

Shortly after Fan Fair ended, *The Woman in Me* reached number one on the country album charts. And it stayed there. With unbelievable speed, she found herself the hottest new act in country music. Just as fast, everyone wanted her: press, TV shows, and concert bookers.

Shania had long been aligned with the Nashville offices

of the international powerhouse Creative Artists Agency. At CAA, the phones began ringing. Since she only had a couple of hit singles at this point, the normal Nashville routine would have been to put her out as an opening act for a major country music star—maybe another high-energy act like Tim McGraw or Brooks & Dunn.

Shania and her manager, Mary Bailey, considered following that path for a while. The artist began discussions with her agent, Ron Baird, who headed the Nashville office of CAA. She had several demands: She wanted to make sure she had first-class lighting, sound, and stage production—something few opening acts receive, much less demand.

As ideas continued to be floated, Shania's stock continued to rise. Not only did she stay at number one, but the gap between her sales and others grew wider. By far, she was the hottest country music act available. Her newly released single, "If You're Not in It for Love (I'm Outta Here)," immediately gained immense attention from radio. But it was only her third hit.

CAA for awhile considered approaching other acts, such long-established stars as Wynonna or Reba McEntire, with the idea of arranging a tour where Shania and the other star would be co-billed. Shania would go on first, but she would receive equal billing in every other way.

Shania gave the idea some thought and presented her reservations. Veterans like Wynonna and Reba have scores of well-known songs to perform; they have veteran, well-rehearsed bands with loads of experience. As much as Shania believed in herself and her ability to win over listeners, she didn't think she was ready yet to put together a show that would compete with the other stars.

"I came to the conclusion that there was no way I was gonna be able to compete show-wise with Reba, Wynonna, (and the others)," Shania later told the *Journal of Country Music*. "If I can't compete with them, then I'm not gonna make an impression. I thought, 'Is there really room for me to get out there and do my thing? How am I gonna stand out above the rest?' Maybe not going out there is the way to stand out above the rest."

For CAA, it was a difficult time; the company only makes money if an artist tours, and the biggest act affiliated with the Nashville office was refusing to go on tour. But Baird didn't try to change Shania's mind. He understood her reasoning, even if he disagreed with it. He didn't try to strong-arm her into making any public appearances or performing any shows. Baird and CAA continued to represent her, even if they weren't getting much return for the time invested.

A backlash against her decision not to tour came in a different, unexpected way. Music critics, as well as many within the music industry, wondered aloud if Shania wasn't a prefabricated creation masterminded by Mutt Lange, her husband, the famous producer who had enacted a Svengali-like influence on other acts in the past.

Few had seen or heard her perform during the Triple Play tour, hardly anyone seemed to remember what she was like on the Disney TV special in which she performed in 1993. Since she started in Canada, no one except Dick Frank and her manager, Mary Bailey, had viewed her Deerhurst Resort shows.

That's when the rumors blew up: She couldn't sing, they said. She was horrible onstage, others said. She's a fake, still more chimed.

As driven and confident as Shania is, she's still sensitive. She has her insecure moments, and listening to talk about how she couldn't perform upset her. Didn't they know she had spent most of her life onstage? Didn't they know that, in truth, she was more comfortable singing live than singing in the studio?

She was anxious to prove critics wrong. But she forced herself to be patient, to not give in solely because of criticism. This was just another trial to get through. She didn't want to give up her plan just to feed her ego or to show others that she loved to perform and was by God good at it, too. She held her ground. She'd show 'em, she thought, when she got the chance. When the time was right. It's just that the right time wasn't right now.

MAYBE SHE WASN'T GOING TO TOUR, BUT THAT doesn't mean she didn't work hard at promoting herself. If anything, Shania continued the standard originally set by Madonna and Mariah Carey on how to succeed enormously in the modern music world without touring.

Like Madonna and Mariah, Shania invested great amounts of effort and money into videos. It was her appearances in videos that had given Shania the most famous bare midriff since Barbara Eden on the '60s TV sitcom, *I Dream of Jeannie*.

Shania never understood the criticism she received for her look in her videos. Now that she had a few hits under her belt, she started speaking out more aggressively against the conservative element that slammed her for selling sexuality rather than music.

"I think that the industry seriously underestimated the fans and where they were at," she said. "I mean, come on, we have the internet these days. Watch TV for an hour! The times are very progressive and very free. That's why I don't particularly pay a lot of attention to what the industry is doing. I don't want to be influenced by it; I don't want to know what they consider right and wrong."

At this point, Shania truly started to break free, to speak her mind without worrying who she might upset. In Nashville, that kind of attitude was rare—and refreshing.

"You can't underestimate or fool the fans," she said. "They live real lives and they want real music, real thoughts, and real words. That's what I try to give them. I like to express to young girls especially that you should feel comfortable with your body. Whether it's an extra roll that you don't like or whatever it is you don't like about your body, you shouldn't feel that you have to hide it."

Of course, not every young girl can spend five hours for a fitting, as Shania did for her video of "If You're Not in It for Love, (I'm Outta Here)." In the video, Shania cavorts with several alternating groups of young, ultra-hip teens and young adults, all of them dancing and playfully fooling around with drums and other instruments.

For the most part, the video pictures Shania exuberantly having fun. But—like her music—it was an excessively expensive and intricately planned performance designed to look as casual as possible. The young girls that Shania says she wants to feel good about themselves don't have all the experts behind them making them look as good as the singer does. That begs the question: Is fooling people into thinking you just wake up, get dressed, and look like she does really the best way to make self-conscious youngsters feel good about their bodies and themselves?

To explain herself, in what would become a common theme, she said, "The best example I can give, because this what I spent doing in my teens, was I had a girlfriend who was very flat-chested, and she could always go around in t-shirts in the summer and in tank tops and stuff like that, and I never felt that I could because I was so heavy-chested," she said. "I covered myself up, and I never went to the beach. Now that I'm older, I'm thinking, what a waste. People should learn to respect the way you look and who you are. Period. I always try to explain to people that it's not about sex. Sensuality is part of being feminine. If you feel that you want to wear something that's sexy, that doesn't mean you're looking for sex. People interpret these things way out of whack. And I think that's just a shame."

In other words, she wasn't going to apologize for acting as sexy as she wanted. She felt the same way about her videos.

"The way I wanted to express myself visually was very overt for country music," she said. "Everybody was saying, 'I don't know. I think you ought to be more conservative.' But that's not how I wanted to be. Even though in the beginning I went against the grain, in the end, it was the best thing I ever did."

Video wasn't her only means of advancing her image, her music, and her career. Unlike her role models, Madonna and Mariah, Shania worked every promotional angle possible, often doing things the other divas would have scoffed at.

In that sense, she followed a pattern set by teen-pop flashes like Tiffany and Debbie Gibson—and one later seized by such current hot teen groups like the Spice Girls, 'N Sync, and the Backstreet Boys.

In other words, Shania worked the media and the crowds without ever performing a song. She appeared everywhere and anywhere that fans would flock or where she could get exposure. From highly advertised autograph signings in malls to special fan-appreciation appearances, from tightly controlled interviews to beautifully airbrushed magazine covers, Shania hit the publicity and promotion trail hard. She tackled each opportunity with the same cool, calculating poise, always smiling with icy consistency. She spun each quote and each photo in a way that worked toward her primary end—to be viewed as a hip, sexy, strong, but down-to-earth gal.

It worked, too. On Feb. 10, 1996—two weeks before the 1996 Grammy Awards at New York's Madison Square Garden—Shania drew 20,000 to an appearance at the Mall of America in Minneapolis. They weren't there to see her perform; they were there just to see her sit and sign autographs.

Such appearances gave Shania and Mercury Records a better idea of who her audience was.

"I get a lot of comments from women who have teenage daughters, and they have turned their daughters onto my music," she says. "I think that's a real compliment when parents and teenagers are listening to the same music."

The creation of her public image became the graphic extension of the creation of the music on *The Woman in Me*. It was carefully and calculating groomed to make her look as natural and as spontaneous as possible.

But Shania repeatedly emphasized that, no matter how important her image and her look on her videos may be, people don't buy CDs because of a picture.

"People are buying my record because of the music," she said firmly. "I haven't had a show, haven't had a tour. That was deliberate. You get an idea from the videos that I'm a very active performer. I didn't want people to think that I'm using the visuals to sell my music."

Well, of course the videos were designed in a way to sell records. What other reason were they produced?

But, she's right in the long run; it's the music that has to hold up. An image only carries a performer for so long. If a listener is going to keep returning, it's because they're singing along. It's because they're hearing something they like.

Meanwhile, amid all this hard work, she found little time to spend with her new husband. Lange hated the spotlight and publicity; he had spent most of his career carefully avoiding being photographed, and he had turned down all requests for an interview or for even a quote about his work or his wife.

But Shania made it clear what her priority was: She was going to do everything possible to keep her career skyrocketing. "She has a very hands-on approach," said John Grady, senior vice president of sales at Mercury Records. "She had all creative control over her music and her videos—over everything. Obviously, the music has to get accepted like everything else, but we did not try and tell her who should produce her record or what it should sound like."

In truth, the company had tried that once before, on her first album. Shania had learned her lesson. With Lange's assistance and counseling, she was now guiding every aspect of her career.

"The videos come from her," Grady said. "She writes a lot of the treatment, and she's involved with the video work right down to the editing. She's even involved in major marketing. I deal with her, not her manager. It's different, but it's refreshing. Shania's keenly interested with how the business works around her music. She doesn't make records for those reasons, but she understands why they work when they get there. She understands the game, but she selects the innings she comes in at. It's all very unique."

For Shania, it was partly a matter of trust. On the first album, she allowed others to tell her what to do. Once she took control, everything fell in line and took off. She would never relinquish control of her career to anyone again.

"At what stage can you let it go and leave it up to somebody else?" she asked. "That's very scary. Now I'm unable to be involved creatively all the way, but I still love it. Being involved is so crucial. Only I can deliver this stuff. I have to follow through with it."

But Shania recruited help when it came to trying to explain herself. As her fame exploded, everyone involved with her career received requests for interviews and comments. Before long, the comments started to sound the same, no matter who did the talking. "This is not a marketing effort," Luke Lewis told an interviewer. "Please, if you're writing about her, it's important that you know that the vision has been hers. She's a total artist, and I'm proud to know her."

In the fall of 1995, Shania crossed the northern border into native country to attend the Canadian Country Music Awards, which were held in Hamilton, Ontario. At that moment, her album had been No. 1 in America for thirteen consecutive weeks—longer than any other woman in country music history.

Michelle Wright, a Canadian singer signed to Arista Records, hosted the event. "It's a girl's night out, eh?" Wright shouted during the show, a reference to the dominating presence of Shania, Wright, and newcomers Terri Clark and Lisa Brokop, both of whom had new country music albums out in America as well as in Canada.

Shania downplayed her hopes at picking up an award—what would be, if she won, the first award of her career. "I don't win awards for a living," she said. "I sing. I'm excited just to be a part of it. Right now, I'm just concentrating on my performance and that's all."

Shania opened the show with a medley of "Any Man of Mine" and "The Woman in Me." But that was just the beginning; she would end up spending most of the evening onstage, picking up award after award. Before the night was over, she would accept trophies for the best single, best video, best album, and best song, as well as for Canada's female vocalist of the year.

"I'm shaking," she told the crowd as the awards began piling up. "I just never thought I'd have so many friends in this world. This is something I've been building up for, for over twenty years."

At the beginning of the awards, Shania bounced onstage, poised as ever, coolly yet excitedly thanking a list of people, Mary Bailey among them. The television cameras zeroed in on Bailey, who provided all the emotion that Shania didn't. Tears streamed down the manager's eyes, the momentous moment pouring through her. After all the years of struggle and hope, Shania indeed had become everything they had hoped she could be.

But by the end of the show, Shania broke down as well. While accepting the female vocalist of the year award, she tearfully dedicated her awards to the two people most responsible for her success—her late parents, Jerry and Sharon Twain. "They can't be here with me," she said, "but they're the reason I'm here."

Within weeks, Shania and Bailey got another jolt of good news: She was nominated for four Grammy Awards, a major boost for someone on her second album.

The scene would be repeated a few months later, when Shania won a Grammy Award for Best Country Album, and in April when the Academy of Country Music Awards gave her awards for best new female vocalist and for the 1996 Album of the Year. At this point, Shania had won every major country music award except those given out in Nashville by the Country Music Association.

As the awards continued to come in, there wouldn't be any more wild emotional reactions. As a youngster, Shania learned to hold her emotions inside. She had gone hungry; she had gone to school with little sleep after a late night of singing; she had kept things together after her parents died. Through all that, she always put up an icily strong front, keeping an even keel while hiding her feelings.

Now that life was much better, now that her dreams were coming true, she acted much the same way. When she won accolades, she put up a strong front, her emotions kept from view. But to some, it appeared as if she expected such fame, fortune, and popularity. She took in stride with such ease that some thought she took it all for granted.

That attitude could be seen most clearly when Shania surpassed Patsy Cline as country music's best-selling female artist of all time. One of country music's most beloved icons, the late Cline had remained a fan favorite for decades. Her legacy only grew stronger after her tragic death by a plane crash in 1963.

But Cline had taken more than thirty years to sell five million albums. Twain did it in ten months. More than that, she became the first country artist to spend fifteen consecutive weeks in the top ten of the Billboard 200 chart, which tracks sales of all genres of music.

For Mercury Records, it was a time of celebration. "We are very proud to be associated with this project," said Luke Lewis, president of Mercury Nashville, the week the album officially topped the five-million mark. "Not only is it great for Mercury Nashville, it is also good for country music in general and female artists in particular."

How did Shania react? "I don't get all that excited," she said. "It's a great thing, but you know what? I don't take a lot of pride in those things for some reason. It just doesn't mean that much."

Her manager, Mary Bailey, got very excited about it. But Shania didn't share Bailey's ebullient excitement about reaching such exalted sales status and breaking such a long-standing record. Shania admits that when Bailey came to celebrate, she wasn't very receptive and certainly wasn't much of a co-celebrant. "I was like, 'That's great. Now let's move on,'" Shania would later say of the momentous moment.

Shania also was starting to make it clear what she meant when she said she wanted to move on. By this point, she already was looking for a bigger world to conquer: pop music.

When speaking to a writer for *Interview* magazine for an article published in March 1996, Shania answered a question about whether she would start directing her music toward pop fans now that she had conquered country music. "I think once you go past selling so many millions of records, you're getting to different audiences outside of country radio," she said. "I keep thinking, 'You don't always know who's buying your records. Are the same people who are buying Alanis Morissette buying Shania Twain, too? You think, 'Where are these people coming from? Because when you start getting into five, six million records, you've got to be overlapping . . . I mean, I'm a country music artist, but what is country music? I think it's a frame of mind, though I think that, to a lot of people, country music is about living the life of a cowboy. I don't want to say that it's not about cowboys, but it's so much more than that."

As might be expected, once Shania became a fast-rising star, the press began to postulate and to probe. As some looked into her past, as they asked about her upbringing, the story of her tragic family background began to circulate.

Shania had never tried to capitalize on the tragedy of her parents' death. She never allowed the public relations staff of Mercury Records to use it to get her into hard-to-crack publications. She made it clear she didn't want the story highlighted in her press information or to be whispered to editors. She wanted to avoid talking about it; she preferred to accentuate the positive.

But when a reporter asked about her parents, there was no getting around it. In such instances, she stuck to facts, speaking as dryly and remotely as possible. She would explain the facts—that her parents had been killed in a car accident when she was twenty-one years old. As more questions followed, she would say that she was able to continue on with her career, and that no, she didn't fall apart.

What happened to the rest of your family, they would ask, to your other brothers and sisters? She would explain that she took care of them. Her older sister had a family of her own by then, she explained. So the rest of the family moved in together, Shania would tell them, and she, as the oldest, became the caretaker.

She explained the circumstances, plainly and straight-forwardly, without emotion. "We just got on with it," she would say, without a hint of tears. She did what she had to do and moved on with her career. She found solace in music, as always. And she concentrated on her career, as always.

Some reporters and music-industry insiders doubted the tale, and Shania's unemotional way of telling the story didn't help. Still, it wouldn't have taken much research for someone to find the facts, which indeed backed up Shania's version. It was true, just as she told it. Still, rumors spread that Shania's story had holes in it, and soon a few journalists and columnists insinuated that Shania wasn't everything she purported to be.

The most public and widely publicized doubter turned out to be writer Laurence Leamer, author of the tell-all book, *The Kennedy Women*. Leamer had penned *Three Chords and the Truth*, a harshly critical book about modern country music. Among other sensational tacks, Leamer suggested that Shania's story was "a brilliant reconstruction . . . a virtual past." He proposed that Shania manufactured her hard-luck story to prop up her image.

However, it ended up that Leamer was the one fabricating an intricate lie. Shania never tried to trade on her past; she only begrudgingly talked about the facts when forced, and she never fell into the usual show-biz dramatics when discussing the difficulties of her youth.

Everything that Leamer accused her of exaggerating turned out to be true: Leamer said she lied when she suggested that Timmins was near the edge of the wilderness; but she's right, it is. Leamer said she never ate wild game as a child; in fact, she did, regularly, thanks to her father's talents at trapping and hunting. Leamer said Shania didn't grow up in a Native-American community; indeed, she did, in Porcupine, on the outskirts of Timmins.

With crass indifference to the truth, Leamer attempted to slander Shania for minor inaccuracies. Because she told one interviewer that her family would go for days on bread and milk, then told another writer that they got by for days on only potatoes, Leamer pondered, "What was it, potatoes or bread and milk?"

Leamer mostly censured her by default. He figured no one lived as poor as she did, so it couldn't be true. "A man could earn a good living in the mines or in the forest if he didn't drink it away on weekends," Leamer wrote, a point a lot of struggling miner's families would love to take up with him. "Didn't Canada have a strong social safety net?"

Leamer didn't bother enough to investigate, just to accuse. In truth, Jerry Twain was too proud to ask for handouts, and he never sought out assistance from social agencies. But Leamer, sounding like Ebenezer Scrooge in *A Christmas Carol*, accused her of exaggerating the impoverished lifestyle of her childhood. In fact, if anything, she downplayed it—a truth Leamer would have discovered if he'd bothered to look into her past at all.

Another purported scandal came up in April of 1996. It originated in Shania's hometown newspaper, the *Tim-*

mins Daily Press, which had been so supportive of her over the years. Again, the news proved to be more vicious than true, but this time it angered Shania more than it hurt her.

"The *Daily Press* has learned that Twain has woven a tapestry of half-truths and outright lies in her climb to the top of the country charts," read the lead front-page story.

In the article, the paper quoted Shania's biological father, Clarence Edwards, who had resurfaced now that his long-lost daughter was famous. He stepped forward to claim his paternal connection to the star, which contradicted Shania's statements that Jerry Twain was her father.

Of course, for all intents and purposes, Jerry Twain *was* Shania's father. At least in her mind he was. He'd married the singer's mother, Sharon, when Shania was two years old. He moved them from Windsor to Timmins and began a life as part of their family. Clarence Edwards, who had abandoned his family, wasn't a part of her life. Jerry Twain was.

At most, Shania was guilty of streamlining her story. She didn't bother supplying her record company with the details of divorce, abandonment, and broken families— all of which happened before she was old enough to remember it. All she knew was of a family life with Jerry Twain, who always did his best to be a good father and husband.

Because Shania became Jerry Twain's stepdaughter so early in her life, and because she had next to no contact with Edwards through her childhood or adult life, it's certainly understandable that, when beginning her career, she simply told interviewers that she was born in Timmins, the daughter of Jerry and Sharon Twain. That's hardly reason to accuse her of weaving "a tapestry of half-truths and outright lies," as the *Daily Press* had done.

The other aspect of the newspaper's exposé, that Shania was not a Native American, was a bit trickier. Still, her explanation is reasonable and rings true. Shania always had said she was partly Indian, that her father Jerry Twain was an Ojibwa Indian, and that she grew up on the Temagami Reserve near Timmins.

Most of that is true: Jerry Twain was an Ojibwa, and the family did live for a while on the reservation. But Clarence Edwards is of French-Irish descent. Her mother Sharon also was Irish. Shania wasn't born in rugged Timmins, but in suburban Windsor.

This all may have been factual, but it wasn't the experience Shania knew. In her mind and in her experience, she was raised in a Native American community near Timmins by an Indian father. With Edwards out of the picture, she fully considered herself the daughter of Jerry Twain, the man who raised her and loved her and cared for her as best he could.

For anyone who grew up under a caring step-parent, especially after being abandoned by the parent who had been replaced, such a scenario is completely understandable. For all intents and purposes, Shania was exactly who she said she was.

Moreover, when her family struggled with poverty and hunger, Edwards was nowhere to be found. When Shania kept her family together after the deaths of Jerry and Sharon Twain, Edwards offered no assistance. However, now that she was becoming an international star, the Edwards family apparently wanted to re-establish ties with the famous singer.

Showing a fire and emotional ferocity missing from her music and her public appearances, Shania shot back with fierce, pointed anger. She didn't give an inch; instead, she vehemently defended the story she had been telling all along.

"I've never had a relationship with my biological father," she wrote in response to the *Daily Press* findings. "Although I was briefly introduced to Clarence a couple of times in my teen years, I never knew him growing up. . . . I never felt the need to seek the love or support of another family because I had it from the Twains."

At the same time, Shania played hardball with the *Daily Press*. She threatened to sue the paper over the allegations, and she withdrew the contract she had with the paper which allowed it to print her fan club newsletter.

The paper responded with a front-page retraction, which ended with the sentence, "The *Daily Press* sincerely regrets any suggestion that Ms. Twain lied."

Later, she would attack Leamer's insulting insinuations about her background with equal fury. "I want to set that guy straight," she told *Rolling Stone*. "Because you know what? The reality is, if anything, I'm easy on the subject. The only reason I talk about it at all is because I have this charity I support (Second Harvest Food Bank's Kid Cafe, which helps feed impoverished children). I want to make people aware of it."

More trouble would rise. Her sister Carrie was arrested for attempting to burn down her boyfriend's home in Timmins. On New Year's Eve in 1996, her half-brothers Mark and Darryl were arrested for driving while intoxicated. The following May, Mark Twain was arrested again, this time for breaking the window of his girlfriend's car during an argument and for assaulting a police officer and resisting arrest, after swinging a loaded backpack at a policeman and hitting him in the face with it.

In a more serious offense, both Mark and Darryl were arrested in Huntsville, Ontario—the town near Deerhurst Resort, where Shania raised them in their later years—and were charged with trying to steal cars. Mark Twain was sentenced to a six-month jail term.

Shania, when queried about the events, always addressed them directly and succinctly. She loved her brothers dearly, she would say. Other than that, it was a private matter, and she refused to discuss it any further.

Still, none of it seemed to affect her too much—neither the success, nor the turmoil. Shania was like a cutter ship, plowing steadily and mightily toward her destination, paying scant attention to the sunny days or the stormy nights.

She acknowledged that some people may see her as cold and calculating. That's not who she is, she said, but she couldn't change people's perceptions. She is who she is: reserved in some ways, but always driving ahead.

"I'm very sensitive in some ways," she said. "I don't come across that way. I tend to be very frank and bold. I'm sure I come across as very driven, very direct, very focused, and none of those things encompass any real sensitivity. But I'm quite a sensitive person."

Meanwhile, none of the publicity did anything to slow her sales. By November 1996, she crossed the ten-million mark, achieving more than double the sales any other woman in country music had ever reached. It also had spent a record twenty-nine weeks at number one on the country singles chart, and twenty-eight weeks in the top ten of the Billboard pop album chart.

As it turned out though, another event that the press largely overlooked said more about the singer's character and sensitivity than any of her family issues.

In late 1996, as she was enjoying the greatest success of her life, she fired Mary Bailey. Both Bailey and Shania had described the singer's longtime friend and mentor as being like a mother to the new star. On the liner notes of her first album, Shania inscribed a special thanks to Mary Bailey, "a true friend and believer; thanks for taking such good care of me all these years."

Shania ended the business relationship with a phone

call and a FedEx package, severing all ties with the woman who had worked so hard and sacrificed so much for the performer. That was that—Shania never called or contacted her again.

Perhaps Bailey should have seen it coming—Shania's career had catapulted to a position where she needed advice and assistance from someone with more experience, connections, and financial support than Bailey could deliver. But Bailey was taken by surprise, and she was shattered.

It didn't take long for Bailey to realize how severe the cut had been. Other stars in similar situations have dealt with their initial managers more tenderly. Some have been absorbed into a larger administrative structure and given a smaller role in a performer's career. Or they were bought out of a contract with a lucrative sum of cash, or given a tiny percentage of future earnings for a certain period of time, in order to compensate them fairly for the time and money they'd invested in a performer when no one else cared about them.

Bailey got nothing like that. She no longer heard from Shania, Mercury Records, CAA, or anybody else. She was cut off completely from the woman she loved and the woman with whom she had shared so many highs and lows.

"I love her talent, I truly do, and I loved her like a child, like a daughter I never had," Bailey told writer Laurence Leamer. "Because of my love, I probably allowed things to happen that, strictly as business, I never would have accepted. I know this industry very well. I looked at her like an athlete going for the gold. When you see people who are that completely focused and determined, they sometimes fail to realize that no one achieves their objectives alone. I understand that."

As well as Bailey may have understood the industry, maybe she was too human, too caring, too involved emotionally to make the cut-throat decisions necessary for someone to get to where Shania wanted to go. In the end, though, Shania's decision hurt Bailey deeply.

"It took a tremendous amount out of me," she admitted. "There are not enough words; it's beyond the call of duty what I did for her and her career. No one can take that away from me. It was not about money. I believed when no one else did, and I mean *no* one. We had some very tough times. People ask me if it bothers me that she never mentions my name and I say no, not at all. I did not become involved for the glory. I did it because I felt the world had to see this exceptional talent. I truly loved her and I have nothing negative to say."

Still, even as she struggles not to criticize her former partner, Bailey's words can't help but paint a picture of someone cold and calculatingly enough to act as Shania did. The singer made no effort to soften or ease the blow or to thank her mentor for all that had transpired.

Without Mary Bailey, it's doubtful Shania would have ever made the leap from Canadian club singer to international superstar. It was Bailey who Shania turned to in the darkest moment of her life, after the death of her parents. It was Bailey who comforted her and who masterminded a way for the young singer to be able to keep performing while raising her younger brothers and sister.

It was Bailey who contacted Deerhurst Resort and, because of her reputation, was able to set up Shania with a job that gave her more than her parents ever did. It was Bailey who knew Nashville attorney Dick Frank, and who he trusted enough to come to Canada to see the young, unknown singer she was so excited about.

For all that, the harshest thing Bailey would say is that she hoped, down the road, that Shania would return to being the caring, loving, thankful person she once knew. "(Shania) has now found happiness with Mutt, as well as overwhelming success," Bailey said. "Through this I hope will evolve the person I know is inside."

Moreover, another comment about Shania by a woman who had known her longer than anyone but family members seems best to describe who Eilleen Edwards Twain Lange is.

"She's very similar to an athlete going for the gold," Bailey said. "I'm sure she's got a frivolous side to her, as I'm sure we all do, but I was never privy to it."

For Shania, Mary Bailey was old news the minute she fired her. When asked about the situation, she responded as if it was too frivolous a question to bother asking. She'd already moved on; why hadn't everybody else?

When questioned about Bailey by the *Toronto Star*,

Shania retorted, "Change is normal. I like to go forward. I'm not a stand-still kind of person. I don't get caught in a comfort zone."

For Bailey, calls continued to come in querying about Shania from those who hadn't or wouldn't have known about the management change. Bailey could do nothing more than refer the caller to Mercury Records. She didn't have a number for Shania's new management company, which happened to be one of the most powerful, most mysterious, and most painstakingly private artist relations companies around.

Landau Management brought muscle, experience, wisdom, and, from a country music point of view, a new level of respect to Shania's corner.

"The reason I chose Jon is that he was very receptive to the direction I was already headed," Shania said. "I wasn't interested in somebody who was going to reinvent my career. He was willing to join, as opposed to take over. There was a mutual respect that I appreciated."

In addition, when looking forward to her long-term goals, which eventually would include mounting enormous world tours, Landau's long-term involvement in Bruce Springsteen's career gave him a level of experience Shania considered valuable.

"His confidence and experience make me feel comfortable that he can do it," she said. "It's a very good relationship."

For Landau's part, he realized that joining Shania after she had sold ten million albums presented a different challenge than working with Bruce Springsteen from the ground-up.

He compared joining her career as jumping onto "the middle of a fast-moving train," Landau said. "People here had already done so much. I just wanted to find ways to add to the situation. She has a wonderful group of people around her doing a great job."

In particular, Landau cited Luke Lewis, the head of Mercury Records in Nashville, as an ally. "Luke has become a close and dear friend of all of us," Landau said.

Shania has since heaped praise upon Landau and his business partner, Barbara Carr. "They were really psyched-up about this project from the time they came aboard," Shania said. "They really changed things and took what I do to another level. They saw what I wanted, and they enabled it to happen. They were much more capable of helping me achieve the dreams and the goals I've wanted to reach. They've helped me tremendously to do what I've done, and I wouldn't have been able to do it without them, I don't think."

BY NOW, SHANIA RANKED AMONG THE BIGGEST acts of the latter half of the 1990s. Of her competition — Alanis Morissette, Celine Dion, Mariah Carey, Hanson — it may have been the Spice Girls who shared the most in common with Shania.

Indeed, more than one commentator has referred to Shania as "country spice." The connections are many: both like ceaselessly perky songs rife with singalong choruses, elementary dance beats, and uncomplicated guitar riffs. Both dress in body-hugging clothes. Both sport carefully designed images blending glamour with earthy vitality and cheeky attitude, and both brandish an ultra-girlish, ultra-cute presence that's a mix of coquettish innocence and flirty suggestiveness.

Clearly, a year or so before five sassy English tarts became the most overexposed English import since Princess Diana, Shania already had adopted a spice-gal strategy to stardom. She bucked convention, using the video screen as her primary marketing tool instead of the tried-and-true concert stage. She expended hundreds of thousands of dollars per clip to present herself posing and twirling, pursing her lips and wiggling her hips, and baring much skin.

There are other corollaries: As with her spicy U.K. counterparts, Shania's breakthrough album was fun in a disposable, guilty-pleasure kind of way, even if the quasi-feminist message of the lyrics didn't quite jibe with the anti-feminist message of her imaging.

In the long run, Shania suggested a woman can be what she wants, what she really really wants, as long as she spends hours getting her hair and makeup just right, wears sexy clothes, and acts like a bouncy, innocent sex object. In videos and publicity photos, which is about the only way the public had seen her at this point, she had been careful to appear vibrant, fashionable, and oh-so-playful.

It all worked wonderfully, of course. Before Shania came along, only three women — Carole King, Whitney Houston, Alanis Morissette — had previously sold more than ten million copies of a single album. Not Celine Dion, not Madonna, not Mariah Carey. Only Shania, Whitney, Alanis, and Carole King. The singer was in elite company.

Chapter Six

Come One, Come All

AFTER *THE WOMAN IN ME* FINALLY DIED DOWN, Shania and Lange bought an enormous spread of land near the Catskill Mountains in the Adirondacks. Their estate covered an amazing twenty square miles, with an electronic security gate at the entrance. The acreage included its own large lake, a vast forest, and a road that wiggles back into the wilderness.

The couple built a giant wooden mansion to their own design, with its centerpiece being a world-class recording studio. The structure, originally intended as a secondary building rather than the main home, also featured guest rooms and business offices for Shania's newly crowned business, Twain Zone. It was very still, very serene, and virtually noiseless, except for the howls and calls of wild animals.

As soon as she settled in, Shania went to work. "I sat down and wrote down the songs and the ideas for the songs that I had," she said. "Then I got with Mutt and collaborated on what we had."

In explaining her writing style, Shania said, "I try and concentrate on what kind of personality do I want to give this idea or that idea. I try and put my thoughts and ideas and lyrics into a form that best expresses the mood and the character I'm imagining. That's what dictates how the songs end up sounding. It dictates everything: How I will look in the photos and how the videos will be written and produced. That's the core of everything: How do I want to present myself? How do I want to present this song?"

Once again, Shania and Lange worked obsessively on creating an album. There was no danger of any creative blocks—the two came up with far more songs than they could ever fit onto one album.

No one from Mercury Records intervened. Free to do as they pleased, they worked faster and with less fuss than on *The Woman in Me*. By late summer of 1997, the couple were staging special listening parties for Mercury Records executives. Everyone involved responded with great enthusiasm to the music they heard.

One carryover from *The Woman in Me* was attitude:

Once again, Shania based a lot of her lyrics on role reversal, on having women say things in ways more often associated with aggressive, outspoken men.

"Obviously, I'm a woman, and women definitely feel these ways," Shania said about her lyrical direction. "But I'm not so sure if women are as bold as to actually speak that way or to act that way a lot of the times. So, yeah, I think there are things that men would say or the way men would think it, but it's a woman saying it. And I am a very frank person. I pretty much get to the point, just in real life, with my own personality. I'm just being myself. I could soften it, sure, but I think it's more fun this way. It's more entertaining this way. I think people will relate to it a lot better instead of finding a roundabout way of saying it."

This time when Shania and Lange buckled down in the studio, it wasn't guesswork—they knew they had an audience. They knew that what they had concocted had worked. This time they just turned everything up a notch.

Shania never sounded pressured or bothered about creating the album. "It happened over such a long period of time, and there was such an overlapping period from the life of the last album to the making of this album, that there was never actually any cut-off point in time when I felt, 'Oh, boy, we gotta get this next record together,'" she said. "It segued quite nicely."

Still, timing aside, the expectations were big. On one hand, Luke Lewis told a reporter that he expected it to sell more than *The Woman in Me*; indeed he expected it to rival Garth Brooks' *No Fences* as the best-selling country album of all time.

Others at Mercury Records sounded more cautionary notes. John Grady, the senior vice president of sales at Mercury Nashville, said, "It's not always easy following up an album as big as her last one. The good news is that they've provided us with an even better record than the last one. She's matured as a vocalist. This is without a doubt the best follow-up record I've heard and one of the most solid records I've ever sold. When you've got sixteen cuts to work with, it's not hard to make a presentation. It's Christmas time, and everything's pointing to this being successful."

Shania breezily denied feeling any burden on her shoulders. "I can't say I'm feeling pressure, but I'm certainly keeping my fingers crossed," she told *Country Song Roundup*. "There are so many new elements to this album, and it's so different that I'm not really putting them up beside each other and hoping to beat the last one in a competitive way—although I do hope that it is successful, or more successful."

The first the public got a taste of the new album came on Sept. 23, 1997, when Mercury Records released the first single, "Love Gets Me Every Time." The single's release was timed so that she could introduce the long-awaited single on the Country Music Association Awards on the night of Sept. 24. The idea was that Shania's millions of fans, eager to hear the new song, would see the performance and contact local radio stations, begging to hear that new Shania Twain song.

The strategy worked. The song broke records right away. In its first week, "Love Gets Me Every Time" entered the *Billboard* magazine country single charts at number twenty-nine, the highest debut single ever for a female country artist and the fourth-highest ever by any country performer.

By the second week, the song leaped to number fifteen, then inched up to number eleven the following week.

Obviously, that response put to rest any fears Mercury Records had about Shania's music being too rock for country radio. Such fears had been pronounced even before the album came out.

Dene Hallam, vice president of programming at KKBQ Houston, told *Billboard* magazine, "I knew I was getting singles from two women superstars the same week, Wynonna Judd and Shania Twain, and I was frightened by the prospects of getting two rock singles. Now, I think it's ironic that the Shania single is much more country than Wynonna's. I'm flabbergasted by that. Shania's song is fabulous; it's very exciting, and it's great for the format."

Luke Lewis, aware that many skeptics still saw Shania as a triumph of a masterful producer and good record company image-making, took the offensive early to try and say it was about the music more than the marketing.

"Thankfully, there doesn't have to be a good marketing spin on this album," he said, adding that the "reaction to the first single has been better than I expected. And the great news is that consumers are already speaking, already reacting to the single."

That theme—that her sales aren't about hype or marketing, but about music—apparently was part of the strategy behind pushing the album from the start.

Any artist who uses her beauty and her body to sell a record as aggressively as Shania did on *The Woman in Me* will have to face comments that the success is about image more than music. The record company wanted to battle that perception.

When an artist's success is based on image, it often leads to a quick burn out. That kind of popularity tends to be youth-based and not to last very long. It will be New Kids on the Block one year, New Edition the next year, Mariah Carey the year after that. Eventually, for an artist to last, they'll need to create music that continues to attract listeners after the short-attention-span fans move onto the next hot new thing.

That obviously fueled Mercury's marketing plan for *Come on Over*: Build Shania as an artist, not an image. Everyone involved with the record was told to use every opportunity possible to put out the message that it's about music, not about marketing.

Lewis's comments aside, a strong marketing plan was in place for *Come on Over*, with extensive media advertising and huge amounts of money and manpower poured into promotion.

With that much muscle pushing an artist and a record, the music industry usually falls into place: radio sees the big bucks coming its way and excitedly puts the record on the air, and retail stores stock plenty of cassette singles in strategic places and hope to start selling the first song to build anticipation for what they hope will be a windfall of profitable sales once the album is released.

This is what the music industry does best: Prepare and respond to sell an album when the artist is already among the hottest properties in the world. Warehouses are stocked, radio excitedly plays the song quickly and regularly, and stores place the CDs on end aisles under banners and cardboard cut-outs of the artist's image. Product is moved.

By Oct. 18, less than a month after the release of "Love Gets Me Every Time," the cassette single had sold 45,000 copies in a seven-day period. It was the second-best selling single that week, nipping at the hem of LeAnn Rimes's smash hit, "How Do I Live."

Within six weeks, the song was number one on the country charts. Her confidence pumped, Shania started thinking beyond the album's release and talking about the impending concert tour—her first as a star.

"Touring was on my mind the whole time I was working on this album," she said. "This is going to be my 'live' album. I was definitely thinking about that, thinking about how exciting the live arrangements would be."

To everyone's delight, "Love Gets Me Every Time"

also entered the pop charts. In only its second week on pop radio, it already had cracked the Top 40 charts, sitting pretty at number thirty-one.

Because the song moved so swiftly up the country charts, Mercury was able to put out the second single, "Don't Be Stupid," to coincide with the nationwide release of the album, which reached eagerly awaiting record stores on Nov. 4.

To support the release of the album, Shania timed her national TV appearance on *The Tonight Show* with Jay Leno for Friday, Nov. 7. She followed that with a Nov. 14 appearance on *Live with Regis and Kathie Lee*, a Dec. 8 guest spot on *The Late Show* with David Letterman, and a Dec. 9 performance on *Good Morning America*.

With "Don't Be Stupid" also getting enthusiastic response, Mercury could tell it had a hit on its hands as soon as it hit the stores. The plan was to continue to push the album for a far longer period than most records.

"There's two years' worth of singles on this album," said Mercury's vice president of promotions, Larry Hughes. Then, following orders to the smallest detail, Hughes added, "In a situation like this, you don't need to hype it. The music literally speaks for itself."

Like the previous album, *Come on Over* gained mixed reviews from critics. Some were harshly dismissive of it, while others praised its pop smarts.

One magazine critic deemed it "artless and calculating," saying it equated being young with being naive and silly. Meanwhile, a newspaper reviewer said it continued to espouse the energetic, independent feel of *The Woman in Me*.

Another critic put it this way, "The come from nowhere success of *The Woman in Me* proved that the world is ready for a combination of traditional instruments, girl-power themes, and dance-pop dynamics. Whether Twain is a modern-day Dolly Parton or a country music Spice Girl is a matter of perspective. But with her third album, she accentuates singalong choruses and simple dance rhythms while downplaying the country elements. As a pop move, it works wonderfully. The emphasis is on fun rather than depth, of course. But no one can accuse her of being stingy: She and her Svengali producer/husband, slick-rock king Mutt Lange, loaded down the album with sixteen songs, all of them quite radio friendly."

The massive number of songs—the most featured on a single country music CD in 1998—indicate how creative Shania felt following the jolt of popularity of *The Woman in Me*.

"It just didn't feel right without any one of those songs," Shania said. "The album just flowed. That was as far as we could narrow it down. I did wonder if we might be throwing away some songs, but I don't ever think you can give the fans too much music."

From the start, Mercury Records made it clear that the company hoped to see Shania enjoy hits on pop radio as well as on country radio. Luke Lewis was talking about that plan even before the album was released.

"Last time we sold a lot of records with eight hits," he said. "But indicators are that there are fewer people listening to country radio now. So, regardless of how successful we are on the radio, we're stepping up our efforts in terms of advertising and being a bit more aggressive with media buys in both print and broadcasting throughout the life of the record."

As successful as "Love Gets Me Every Time" and "Don't Be Stupid" were, it was the third single, "You're Still the One," that really set the album on its course. The sweet, mid-tempo pop song reached number one on the country charts and number two on the single charts simultaneously in May. It also hit number one on adult contemporary radio, which meant that the song was receiving airplay on three different formats.

Meanwhile, MTV, VH-1, CMT, Canada's Much Music—indeed, every major video outlet in North America—was playing the song's sexy video. A song couldn't have received more exposure than that, and fans responded by giving Shania's album another sales jolt. At this point, the album had been out more than six months, and sales momentum was still climbing.

Most of the hit songs from *Come on Over*, at least through 1998, concentrated on the lighter side of Shania's songs. But she occasionally tackles more substantive themes as well. For instance, her song "If You Want to Touch Her, Ask!" from *Come on Over*, drew on a discomforting aspect of her youth.

"I developed real young as a girl," she said in a theme

she constantly raises in interviews. "The reality is that I went through a lot of anger and frustration over that as a teenage girl. The guys see a girl who's developed up there, maybe they touch you up there and you really feel invaded. And so, you know what? The easiest thing is to just cover them up, trying to get rid of the bounce factor. And that's what I did. I wore three shirts at a time. I tied myself in."

How Shania dealt with the topic offered insight into how she thinks music can help with serious subjects. As she explained, "I could have made it a much deeper, darker song. But that's not the way I go."

Instead, she turned the song about young boys violating girls into a peppy, singalong ditty—complete with an exclamation point.

"I prefer to deal with serious subjects in a lighthearted manner," she said. "I think that helps people get past them. I don't want to dwell on the negative aspect. What I want to do is give girls the encouragement to deal with it in a positive way, to deal with it from strength, not from weakness."

Her manager, Jon Landau, understands that, and he applauds it. "I think her approach to her life experiences is to strive for a kind of positiveness that animates most of what she writes," he said. "I think that's her philosophy . . . To me, she is utterly real."

Clearly, although she wasn't willing to admit it until later, Twain recorded *Come on Over* with an eye on the pop audience. By the time she was featured on the cover of

Rolling Stone in September 1998, she would openly admit that she didn't think of herself as a country artist or a pop artist, but simply as an artist with global aspirations.

She had done "whatever it took to get work," she said, apparently including coming to Nashville as a means to establishing a career. But she'd always held onto a larger dream. "My goal has always been to be international," she said. "It's what I have wanted right from the start."

She had always used a pop approach to music anyway. She wrote songs that were catchy and clever, and she desired to make them as commercial and popular as she could—rather than expressing some hidden darkness, like Nirvana or Pearl Jam, or angering and offending folks like Marilyn Manson and Nine Inch Nails. And, like many pop stars, she used her looks to give her songs more appeal and to draw attention to her music.

Twain suggests country radio led the way to her efforts to crossover to the pop audience. Country radio broadcasters were the first to ask her for special dance mixes, and she and Lange responded with pepped-up versions of "If Youre Not in It for Love (I'm Outta Here)" and "Any Man of Mine." "Right then and there, we knew this was for lots of listeners," she said of her music.

As she had said before, she'd always listened to all styles of music, no matter the genre. She returned to that theme again as she started getting asked about having her music played on more than one radio format.

"That's the way I've always seen music," Shania said.

"Since I love all kinds of music, it really pleases me that I get a chance to access all the fans out there. I get a real thrill out of that, thinking I'm reaching fans who listen to all different kinds of music."

She acknowledged that sometimes having a broad-based sound can be detrimental to a performer. In modern music, songs are directed at niche marketing groups—country, rock, soul, jazz. Crossing styles can make it hard to get support from any one of the divisions.

"I know my music is difficult to categorize," Shania said. "I know that can be difficult for a record company to sell or for a radio station to accept. But being different and original is also the very thing that makes my music successful. And I appreciate the people who support my ideas and those who are willing to take a risk to play them."

Once she gained a chance to be heard on various radio stations, she said she couldn't have asked for a better opportunity. "I've found a place where I can reach all the fans, which, for an artist, is so important," she said. "It's so sad to be limited to who gets to hear you. I think that's such a terrible thing, artistically, that that could happen to anyone."

As had happened in the past, the only snag confronted by "You're Still the One" was from the conservative country element that protested the sexy scenes in the song's video.

"It's totally ridiculous if anyone thinks I'm pushing the limits with that video," she said. "There is nothing revealing about it. I'm wrapped up to the gills. The video is sensual and has a surreal feel about it, but there is nothing sexual about it. When you start kissing and touching, it's sexual. But sensual? That's fine, in my opinion—it's a very romantic song."

Meanwhile, after Shania found some success on the pop charts, other country performers began to receive airplay on pop stations, too.

That movement greatly excited the country music industry. The reasoning went like this: If country music accounts for fourteen percent of all U.S. album sales while limited to airplay on one radio format, how big might the future be if the music begins reaching the larger audience afforded to pop singers, most of whom enjoy radio play on a variety of formats?

"This does feel like a breakthrough," said Luke Lewis. "It reminds me of the early '80s, when Michael Jackson's *Thriller* broke down barriers for black musicians on MTV and on pop radio. Now that pop radio has seen how listeners respond to LeAnn (Rimes) and Shania, they're ready to try more of it."

So far, the benefits have been great for both camps: Those artists getting pop radio play—Shania, LeAnn Rimes, Faith Hill, and others—saw their sales skyrocket as a result; meanwhile, radio stations found that airing select country songs livened up their playlists and increased their listener base.

"Top 40 has always been the best of all genres," said John Ivey, program director of Boston's leading pop station, WSKS-FM (Kiss 108). "We should play whatever the best available records are. I think all of the songs we're talking about are great songs. To me, they all sound like pop, and they've been big records for us."

Lon Helton, country music editor of the broadcast trade magazine *Radio & Records*, said at least eight hits in 1998 began on the country music charts and then crossed over to get airplay on adult-contemporary radio. Three of those songs—Shania's "You're Still the One," LeAnn Rimes' "How Do I Live," and Faith Hill's "This Kiss"— gained widespread success at Top 40, or "contemporary hits radio," as well.

"There's more crossover music coming out of country than at anytime in the past," Helton said. "I don't remember it ever being this massive—not even in the 'Urban Cowboy' days. To have so much happen in such brief period of time really is unprecedented."

What's remarkable is the movement's broad scope: In addition to Shania, Rimes, and Hill, those gaining significant airplay on adult-contemporary radio stations included Garth Brooks, JoDee Messina, Alan Jackson, and Martina McBride. In the past, country-to-pop crossover hits were usually isolated incidents, when songs like Marty Robbins' "El Paso," Roger Miller's "King of the Road," Dolly Parton's "9 to 5," or Willie Nelson's duet with Julio Yglesias, "To All the Girls I've Loved Before," enjoyed success on both charts.

Jim Ed Norman, longtime president of Warner Bros. in Nashville, wasn't surprised at the success. "I think we've been given a shot, and that's all we really needed," he said. "Given the chance, we can show that we have great music that can compete with music from other genres."

So far, most of the pop radio play has gone to female country singers and to songs with a distinctly pop edge. Part of the reason is that most male country singers wear cowboy hats, boots, and other items that strongly identify them with rural Southern culture.

"I'm not sure pop listeners are ready to have people with cowboy hats on their format," said Chris Stacey, senior director of national promotions of Mercury Records.

The last time pop radio blended country songs into its playlists was in the late '70s and early '80s, when hits by Eddie Rabbitt, Kenny Rogers, Crystal Gayle, and Willie Nelson were aired in sequence with popular records by the Eagles, Linda Ronstadt, and Boston.

However, beginning in the '80s, pop radio took on a harder-edged sound. As the pop format turned toward rap and hard rock, country songs no longer fit into the format. But the recent rise of melodic hit songs by the Wallflowers, Jewel, and Hootie & the Blowfish, as well as Nashville's new emphasis on youthful performers, led to the sounds of country and pop coming closer together again.

"It's easy for radio to play LeAnn Rimes after Celine Dion, or Shania Twain after Mariah Carey," said Mike Curb, head of Nashville-based Curb Records. "It fits."

Chris Stacey of Mercury Records thought the appeal

extended to how the singers looked as well as how they sounded.

"Shania has an image that transcends boundaries and formats," Stacey says. "She's a beautiful, energetic woman who appeals to younger listeners, and that's what pop music has always been about."

Though Shania occasionally received pop radio airplay on previous songs, it wasn't until "You're the Still One" that she was fully accepted by pop stations.

"Shania obviously wants to be a big star," Stacey noted. "And she's certainly got the stuff to do it. She's selling huge numbers of records. I don't see why any format wouldn't want to deal with her."

What's different about the current crossover movement is that it's not gaining resistance from country radio programmers. In the late '70s, Dolly Parton, Willie Nelson, and others were penalized by country radio for cross-marketing songs to different formats. So far, country radio has continued to embrace Shania, Rimes, Hill, and the others.

"It's been 180 degrees different from how they reacted during the Urban Cowboy era," said *Radio & Records'* Helton, who talks daily to country radio programmers across the United States. "Twenty years ago, the stations were real upset about it. Now they see it as a commercial for their station and for country music."

As Helton and many in the country music industry saw it, a listener can hear one song by Shania on a pop or adult-contemporary station, but they can hear several more by her on country radio. Moreover, if a listener scanned across the dial and heard a Shania song on country radio, they'd stay. Afterwards, they might hear another song they'd like and start visiting the station more often.

"Country radio has been losing listeners in the last couple of years," Luke Lewis said. "For Shania to fulfill her promise, it's our duty to take her out and expose her to as many people as we possibly can. We're doing that. But, for country radio, what we're doing is grabbing people with good music and bringing them back."

Meanwhile, many Nashville executives salivate at the possibilities of seeing more country records played on more than one radio format.

"It's always been about access," said Jim Ed Norman of Warner Bros. Records. "A singer like Faith Hill or Shania Twain has all the qualities and meets all qualifications that would be expected to make it in the pop marketplace. All it takes is for the programmers to have the openness it takes to give singers like that a chance. Give them a chance, give them that exposure, and they're going to be embraced."

However, some portions of country radio did protest. So did other country-based media. Janet Williams, a reporter with *Country Weekly*, asked Shania during a press conference why she had abandoned the country media once she was famous. Williams pointedly asked Twain if she would ever come back and appear on shows like the Nashville Network's *Prime Time Country*, since she was quick to appear on the show when she needed them but had turned down requests after becoming famous.

Shania's answer was typically direct. She could've blamed a lack of time, for example, but she didn't.

"I gave four years of my life to promotion and publicity," Shania said. "I worked a lot harder on it then than I do now, and that was harder work than what I'm doing now. Now I go out and have a ball expending all the energy I can for two hours every night. That's easy for me, but it's where all my focus is. That's what I'm concentrating on. It is a two-hour show. It's physically demanding. Once the tour is over, then maybe I can get back to do more publicity and promotion again."

As "You're Still the One" finally started to fade from the airwaves, Mercury Records made the unusual move of sending out two different singles simultaneously.

At the same time as "Honey I'm Home" was sent to country radio, she shipped the power ballad, "From This Moment On," to pop and adult-contemporary radio stations. That was a first for her—separating songs from her album for the country market and the pop market.

"From This Moment On" wasn't a song she planned to sing when she first wrote it. She didn't think it would be right for her. A power ballad that could use a big, strong voice, Shania originally thought she might pitch it to another singer, such as her Canadian pal, Celine Dion.

Listening to "From This Moment On," it's obvious she attempted to write a ballad custom-made for weddings and at proms. In the song's introduction, Twain promises,

"Through weakness and strength, happiness and sorrow, for better, for worse, I will love you with every beat of my heart."

As she explains, it, "I started writing 'From This Moment On' without even thinking it would be on the album," she said. "It's one of the songs that I hadn't seen for myself until the last couple of months before recording the album. I think you do just go through a period of being creative. You don't necessarily say, 'I'm going to write sixteen songs for the next record, and this is what they're going to be about.' It's very much a slower, much more organic process. And even the amount of songs that are on the album, we didn't decide that until very close to the time of recording. We kept narrowing the list of songs down that we were going to complete and refine and rewrite, and we never got any lower than sixteen So we just kept it at that."

That duality, sending songs to both the country and pop market, suits her sensibilities. "My influences are so much broader than (just country music)," she said. "I'd have to say that the base is definitely country, that's just because I started singing country so young, and that's all I sang for so long. I think I was sixteen years old before I started singing any other kind of music live. But I always listened to many different styles of music that would come out of my songwriting. So even from the age of eight, I was writing songs that could be considered more pop and R&B, and there were country ones, too. So I think that there are influences from everything in the music.

It's kind of shown in my fan base. There's such a wide range of listeners."

Meanwhile, the commercial endorsement offers started pouring in once Shania enjoyed pop success. She became a celebrity model for Candies shoes and Gitano jeans — two youth-oriented products.

But, even with this widespread success, she assured her country fans that she wasn't jetting off in a new direction. "I'm not leaving country music," she said. "The majority of what's going on for me is in country, and probably always will be. I don't see that changing."

Her appearance on the cover of *Rolling Stone* magazine was another benefit of her pop success. She became the first female from country music to be shown on the cover since Dolly Parton's appearance in 1980.

The cover was designed to turn heads. Shot in an open field in Ohio, the cover photo shows Shania in black leather hip-hugger pants. A silk scarf barely covers her breasts; it looks as if it is about to blow away and Shania has reached out to try and catch it.

Rolling Stone readers protested, not about the racy shot but about the idea of putting a country music star on the cover of a rock 'n' roll magazine. One letter writer, Michael DeAntonio from South Carolina, said he didn't protest when *Rolling Stone* started covering rap, and he kept quiet when sports started getting extensive coverage in the magazine. "But country music?" he asked.

Another letter pointed out that the issue's other major story was on fast food and then drew comparisons between Shania and drive-through dinners. Her "calculatedly packaged, inspiration-free music does more to flatten and homogenize our cultural landscape than any burger chain ever could," the letter said.

A third letter was more understanding. It thanked the magazine for telling Shania's inspirational story, adding "she is beautiful inside and out."

In Nashville, the complaints were directed at the photograph more than at the magazine. A newspaper columnist quoted women on Music Row as saying that Shania's eyes looked cold and distant; another compared her face to that of a rat or ferret.

Shania defended the cover photograph, telling a Nashville newspaper reporter, "There's absolutely nothing revealing about that photograph, and that's the point. It isn't revealing at all. In fact, it's even less revealing than if I was in a bathing suit top. There's zero cleavage. There's absolutely nothing showing."

The argument was the same one used to defend her videos, that her appearance was slyly sensual, not overtly sexual. "There's nothing wrong with a suggestion," she said. "I almost find that sexier. If you look at all the old movies, it's almost more exciting to watch people almost kiss than it is now to watch movies where they're just naked all over the place. That's what I'm more drawn to. I think that's more sensual and it's more decent."

Besides, she added, she doesn't give a lot of thought to photo shoots anyway. "It's not that tough, and it's not all that thought out," she said. "You go to where they tell you to go and there's a rack of clothes, you put on something, and they take photographs. I don't make a big deal out of it. I try to have fun and relax and look my best, but it's not something I spend a lot of time worrying about. I just go with the flow."

By September of 1998, as Shania prepared to appear on the Country Music Association Awards program, her sales crossed the five million mark. *Come on Over* was clearly a success. At a time when every other country star—even Garth Brooks—was experiencing a drop in total sales per album, Shania was keeping pace with the remarkable sales of her previous album. At that moment, she was country music's biggest seller and its hottest star.

Moreover, the album was selling stronger than ever, even though it had been in record stores for more than ten months. By November, it had spent more than fifty weeks on the *Billboard* chart. At about the same time, it experienced another sales surge, climbing from number seven to number three on the album sales chart. While such high-profile stars as Marilyn Manson, Hole, and Alanis Morissette faced disappointing sales, Shania remained strong.

By now it was clear, she was more than the biggest artist in country music. She was the most consistently successful pop music artist of 1998.

At the BMI party in Shania's honor in Nashville in September, Mercury Records and Landau Management toasted each other's success while praising their artist. "We've sold the first five million albums without a single argument, although you'd think from time to time we should be having some," Landau said. "The whole team is very much in sync. It's been a great experience."

When it came time for her to speak, Shania joined the chorus of those handing out compliments. "Every single person at Mercury Records had been tremendously supportive," she said. "There are no yes men. I've challenged them and they responded with the right things at the right times and in the right places. They don't always tell me what I want to hear, but what they tell me is always in my best interests. You should be proud of what you've accomplished. It's a tough industry, and it's getting tougher all the time. I'm glad to have you on my side."

Shania also referred to her husband, calling him "the other half" of the equation. "Without him, I wouldn't be standing here at all," she said. "He teaches me every day to believe in myself. The bigger you get, the harder it is to get to the next step. He holds my hand and gives me such great support and encouragement and advice."

Still, she admitted, Lange's role in her career also will always cast a certain shadow on what's been created: How much of it is her and how much is it him?

Shania realized this, and she hopes someday to be accepted as the creator of her own kingdom.

"Definitely the people around me and everybody who knows me realizes how much I contribute to my career," she said. "I really do play the role of being the leader of the pack. I definitely am the spearhead to what happens in my career in so many ways, in everything I do. But, yes, there are those behind-the-scenes things that of course the industry and fans don't necessarily get to see. So yeah, I tend to be a little misunderstood at times, because my image is very playful and light and fun and entertaining—which is my goal. I think it just takes time for people to get educated about how much I really do contribute to my career and my music. I think it's something a lot of people don't give me credit for just yet."

Chapter Seven

A Diva, After All

FOR ALL OF HER SUCCESS AS A RECORD SELLER,
Shania knew that she would never be taken seriously
until she proved she was as popular onstage as she was
on record.

As she prepared to begin her debut concert tour in
1998, she made it plain why she chose to move her management from her mentor Mary Bailey to the high-powered firm of Landau Management.

"It's the experience I appreciate more than anything,"
she said of working with Jon Landau and Barbara Carr.

"Like going into this type of touring, for instance, is a first for me, in this environment, and you really want to have somebody who's been there, done that—especially on a level that Springsteen has. So you're getting somebody who knows what they're doing, and it's a great relief, 'cause I want things to be big, and a lot of people that are that big, most of them are in pop. Garth is one of the few exceptions in country. He may be the only exception in country."

Shania prepared as best she could for her introductory arena show. She staged auditions at an arena near Lake Placid, N.Y. that is usually used for ice skating. She bought a luxury bus and hired an expert craftsman to custom-design the interior.

Once she hired her band, she set up for rehearsals to begin at the same Lake Placid ice arena. Then she hired a bus driver; for the month of April, his job would be to drive Shania the short distance from her Catskills home to the nearby arena.

At long last, Shania would be onstage, without Lange standing between her and her listeners. It was something she desperately wanted to happen. But, now that was the time was near, she was calm and matter-of-fact.

She even showed empathy for all of those who had criticized her or suggested she was a fraud.

"I would have been very naive to not have expected that, because I was the only one, practically, not doing it," she says of touring. "Mariah Carey's the only other person, really, who's ever done that in recent years. I mean, it's unusual to not support yourself with a tour, but I really can do it."

She admitted that the criticism tried her patience. But, at this point, she was proud that she stayed the course.

"When you become a celebrity through just your records and there aren't any performances at all to support it, then you're going to get blasted, I guess," she said. "But it's hard to sit back and listen to people criticize who don't really know what you're really about."

Once again, the troops formed. Marching orders were given. And the front line of Team Shania walked forth and spoke in her defense.

"It's a shame for her to have to face this kind of pressure," Luke Lewis said. "But one of the admirable things is how well she's taken it and not complained or altered her vision. That says a lot about her. Now, when people see this show, it will blow them away, and all the critics will be proven wrong. It will all go away once people get a chance to see her. They'll see she's a true, whole, well-rounded artist."

Her long-suffering concert booking agent, who until this point had one of the world's biggest stars on his roster but had yet to be able to really go to work, was perhaps the most eager of all to have Shania prove her doubters wrong.

"It's understandable that people, having never seen her or having extremely limited views of her live performance, could wonder, 'Does she really sing well?,' " said Ron Baird of Creative Artists Agency. "The answer is about to be delivered in a very, very big way."

HER SUMMER CONCERT TOUR OF 1998 PROVED her carpers wrong, city by city. Sure, she was far from pop music's most capable vocalist. Sure, her songs were frothy ear candy designed to entertain rather than enlighten. But, night after night, she ended her shows to raucous standing ovations.

Whatever critics thought of her music, they couldn't say she didn't perform with heart, energy, and style. And they could no longer say she couldn't do onstage what she did in the recording studio—that is, find a way to make music that pleased crowds of people.

She even tried to win over those who said she didn't write about important, real-life issues. Each night, she introduced her song "Black Eyes, Blue Tears" as her attempt to encourage battered and abused women to seek help and to leave bad situations.

Her way of going about this might sound superficial— "Black eyes, don't need 'em!"—she sings in the song's chorus. But her encouragement and motivation were real and heartfelt, she said.

Again, she wanted to give women a positive anthem, one that focused on action rather than on reliving the violence they'd endured. While on tour, she heard from women who said the song was the reason they'd finally left an abusive relationship. That was all the support Shania needed to keep highlighting the song in her shows.

She also often opened her song "God Bless the Child" with a speech about the Second Harvest Food Bank and its Kids Cafe program, which is designed to feed impoverished children.

"I grew up a hungry kid, so I know what it's like to go to school without breakfast or enough money for lunch, and to go home and not have a dinner like the other kids," Shania said. "Of course it goes unnoticed, because people have pride and they hide it. We're all very good at hiding things because of pride. I hope programs like this can help make sure that no kid ever has to go hungry again."

Similarly, she brought out a young local girl to sing during her show at every concert stop. The girl, usually someone who won a local talent contest sponsored by a radio station, would join Shania onstage to sing her first single, "What Made You Say That."

To explain why she put this segment in her concert, Shania said, "I started out singing at clubs as a young child of eight, and that's why I like to bring kids out in my shows. Because I was only able to start singing because bands would invite me up. I realize how much this means to them."

Another important aspect of her concert was the multi-gender, multi-cultural makeup of her band. With three fiddlers and three guitarists, the eight-piece backing group was larger than the average country or pop music touring unit.

There was no other band like it on the road in 1998: The band had Americans, Canadians, Australians, and Brits; it had women and men, and whites, blacks, and Asian-Americans.

For all that diversity, Shania preferred to concentrate on talking about their abilities. "It was hard to find musicians who could live up to the standards set on the record," she said. "I have the best band in the world right now, there's no doubt about it. Every night, they're very challenged by what I ask them to do musically. They've been up to the challenge every night."

The concert tour was an enormous success, on every level. Shania sold out all twelve of her Canadian dates the day tickets went on sale. The same response followed when she crossed the border into the northern part of the United States, in cities that aren't considered country music hotbeds.

Nonetheless, she sold out concerts within hours of tickets going on sale in Spokane, Salt Lake City, and in Milwaukee. She sold out Detroit's Pine Knob Theater in twenty-nine minutes; only the Who, Metallica, and Bob Seger had sold out with similar abruptness.

The tour faced its occasional unplanned problems. At the New York State Fair, a thunderstorm blew through the outdoor arena after Shania went onstage. The crowd of 16,800 stayed despite heavy rain and high winds. But when lightning struck forty yards behind the stage, Shania ended the show.

But mostly it was smooth and triumphant throughout North America for the singer, with sell-outs everywhere.

Some of the country's toughest music critics also came around to praising her.

Jon Pareles, chief pop music critic of *The New York Times*, wrote, "Shania Twain is a rebel. She sings about taking charge and about unabashed lust."

Richard Harrington in the *Washington Post* exclaimed, "Twain clearly had the presence, the charm, the songs, and the support—the total package."

And Greg Kot in the *Chicago Tribune* offered, "Twain kept the buzzing big-beat hooks coming . . . devoting most of her two-hour performance to rocking singalongs . . . she projected a no-nonsense determination as she two-stepped across the three-tiered stage."

Shania shrugged off such comments with the same aplomb with which she handled everything.

"People thought I was going to be petrified and that it was going to be a disaster," she said. "Meanwhile, it's the easiest part of anything that I've ever done. The irony is that the studio and video and television—all the controlled environments that were very new to me a few years ago—that's the stuff I was most uncomfortable with. When you go up onstage in front of a live audience, the freedom is unbelievable. And when you're on television in a video, or in the studio, you have to achieve communication without communicating."

She even met her detractors halfway, admitting that her voice may not be as capable as some others, but her emphasis was on entertainment and energy.

"If I wanted to get a perfect vocal—not miss a beat, not miss a word, not miss a note—I wouldn't be able to be as energetic as I am onstage," she said. "It's a bit of a compromise, but there's no way I could get up there night after night and not give an energetic performance. If I'm not sweating it out and breathing heavy, I'm not working hard enough."

DESPITE ALL THE INTERACTION WITH CHILDREN and choirs during her concerts, Shania did little to warm up her image as a cool, aloof character as she traveled across the United States. Various attempts at finding a bodyguard in the previous few years had failed. She didn't like someone that close to her, that constantly in touch, that totally involved. She preferred privacy, solitude. She preferred to be alone.

So her two constant companions became a watchdog and her horse. Though neither animal was well-suited to travel, Shania took them along to keep herself happy. Tim, her German Shepherd, was of a special breed, a Shutzhund-trained dog who had been taught to be intently loyal to one person. If Tim was in the room with Shania, he was next to her.

As for her horse, it's an Andalusian named Dancer from Shania's home stable. A trainer transports Dancer from city to city, arranging a pasture and a barn for him to stay at each brief stop.

"He's a very experienced traveler," she said. "It'll be great for me to have him there."

She designed the bus so that Tim had his own door for entering and departing. She also had it custom-designed so that it had a bigger than average bed for a tour bus, as well as a full bathtub and a miniature rehearsal studio. "It's more like a cabin than a luxury apartment," she added.

She also had the designers install a kitchen that was bigger than the company had ever put into a tour bus.

"I plan to eat a lot on my bus," Shania told *Country Weekly*. "I love baths, and I want to maybe record a few things that I write, so it's set up more like a living room. I've got the doggie hatch so I can let the dog in and out without having to go outside—little things like that. It has two doors, so I have my own private living area. I know what it's like to live on a bus, and I know where I want things, so I've rearranged it the way I want it."

That sense of comfort and convenience are more important to Shania than ornate luxury or showy items. To her, fame isn't about wealth and glamour, but about hard work and presenting herself the way she desires.

"I'm not really experiencing fame," she said. "I didn't know what to expect, to be honest. I did think it would be more glamorous. I always thought it would be fun to have somebody doing your hair and makeup every day, and somebody shopping for your clothes. I thought it would be fun to sit around and drink tea and pick through clothes. Let me tell you, it's not like that at all. It's more like, 'You've got five minutes, and you better look great.' It's not this wonderful, glamorous experience I toyed with in front of the mirror as a child."

AS IF SHANIA NEEDED ANOTHER SIGN OF TRI-umph, she was among the handful of vocalists invited to take part in a high-profile concert sponsored by the VH-1 cable channel and featuring several of the biggest names in music.

Onstage at New York City's Beacon Theater, Shania was all business—as always. Before the cameras came on, she checked her stage cues, went over the camera an-gles, and argued about lighting and how much time she had for the show.

But she also took a moment to bask. The banner hang-ing behind the stage, VH-1 Divas, told part of the story. Not only were Shania's videos now gaining access to video and radio formats previously denied country stars; now she was getting invited to take part in television spe-cials presented by pop-based video cable channels.

The lineup for the *VH-1 Divas* concert proved how es-teemed the Shania name had become. That night, she would join Mariah Carey, Celine Dion, Gloria Estefan, and legends Aretha Franklin, and Carole King in a televised special that would be seen by millions. A best-selling CD and video would follow.

To Shania, and to everyone else, the billing said one thing: That she was among the biggest music stars in the world.

But there were questions, always questions. One New York columnist questioned what a lightweight teeny bopper like Shania was doing amid the powerful voices of Dion, Carey, and Franklin?

But the fact that Shania performs upbeat, dance-flavored pop music with a country flavor actually ended up giving her a unique feel during the concert and video. While Dion and Carey battled it out to see who could sing the loudest and hold notes the longest, Shania simply came out smiling, bouncing around the stage and energizing the New York crowd with her accessible, fun songs.

There were many who thought she might stumble in such company, that her talent would be revealed as flimsy among such notable vocalists. Instead, she proved that pop music is as much about attitude as skill; the crowd clearly had a ball when Shania was onstage.

"It was an amazingly difficult and pressure-filled position that she totally pulled off," said Ron Baird of the Creative Artists Agency.

Shania, as usual, took her victorious performance in stride. She acknowledged that she did a good job, then went back to work.

"What anything like that does for me is just remind me that the boundaries are not as strong as the industry wants them to be," she later told an interviewer. "It's great to be able to break free of the labels once in a while and just be one of the great artists. That's all you ever want to be: one of the great artists of your generation."

BY THE FALL OF 1998, AS SHANIA REMAINED AT the front of the biggest tour of the year, she nonetheless showed a restlessness offstage. Shania and her husband decided to sell their 3,000-acre mountain ranch in upstate New York, although they'd bought it less than four years earlier.

"I didn't have to move," Shania said. "We decided to sell the studio and to build a place to live and work where we could do what we want."

Many neighbors and local leaders said they'd be sorry to see the couple go.

"She was really good to the town, our fire department, the senior citizens," Franklin Country Legislature chairman Ray Susice told the local paper, the *Plattsburg Press-Republican*. "And she gave a lot of work to the people in the surrounding area."

But Shania and Lange planned to move their studio and their primary residence to Switzerland. They also would maintain a home in Southwestern Florida, and

Shania repeatedly said she'd like to buy a cabin on a lake in Northern Ontario.

"I really miss Canada," she said. "I really miss my family. We're thinking we'll but a little cottage up north near the area where I'm from."

In the end, what both Shania and her husband seek the most is to be away from troubles and from people. Just as her husband likes his privacy, Shania wants to be removed from the bother of populated areas.

"I like small places," she said. "I like a simple life, and I like being in my own environment."

Shania's fame had grown to the point that she had now become fodder for the tabloids and the paparazzi. Neither of them wanted that kind of intrusion, so they decided to remove themselves as much as possible from society.

"I mean, look," Shania explained. "I live in the most remote area you could possibly live in, and yet everyone knows everything about me. I come into town wearing a hat and sunglasses, and I'm still recognized. It must be my mouth or something. Anyway, you just want to be one of everybody else. Especially me. I know I'll get more privacy over there; it'll be nice to be able to get on a plane and get off and then be in a completely different world. Because of the type of person I am, I'll enjoy that."

Moreover, there have been suggestions that Shania's next step will be to move not just beyond country music, but beyond music and into new areas of entertainment.

Her agent, Ron Baird of CAA, says acting is a strong possibility.

"She's one of the most focused artists I've had the pleasure of working with," he said. "We've had so many opportunities over the success of these last two albums, I can't begin to tell you the headline roles she's been offered in featured movies with major co-stars."

Unlike others who've moved beyond country music to tackle bigger worlds, Shania will not be restrained by her beginnings. She'll have no problem moving beyond any identification with the South or with rural communities, because her personality is free of any regional flavor.

Dolly Parton, another country singer who conquered the world, couldn't wash the country off her if she tried. Everything about Dolly reeks of rural, Southern life, and she doesn't try to be anything different.

Garth Brooks will be forever identified with the hat he donned when he hit Nashville. Originally his oversized cowboy hat served as a marketing tool, but now it marks him in a way that many rock and pop fans will have trouble getting past.

Shania is just the opposite—she never really seemed like a country music artist in the first place. Maybe that's why Nashville has always treated her with suspicion. Even though she can ride a horse, even though she occasionally dons a cowboy hat and plaid shirts, no one is going to mistake Shania for a backwoods country gal.

She's hip, she's progressive, and even if she can wield a chainsaw and trap wild game, she nonetheless has the athletic appeal of someone who grew up in malls and watching sitcoms and videos. Her audience can look at her and want to be her; that's not something rock or pop fans do when they look at Dolly, Reba, or Garth.

Talking about the negativity toward her that seems to exist in Nashville, Shania said, "I didn't realize I was going to be such a little stinker. I mean, a lot of people really thought I shouldn't be let loose. Afterward, I stayed in my own world. I stopped listening to country music. I just wanted to give the fans more of what they liked and enjoyed."

As a child, she said, her dream wasn't to be a big star. She wanted to be a songwriter, she said. And, despite all the glory and attention, she still considers her songs as her greatest strength.

"My original dream was to be in the background," she said. "I've been a closet songwriter for a long time, until my parents forced me to play music. Being a star is a fleeting thing. Being a songwriter is forever, even if you just do it for yourself."

Now that she's made it, she says she knows what paved her way—her songs. It's not her beauty, her sexy videos, or the production techniques of her famous husband.

"Look at my first album," she said. "My image was exactly the same then as now. I didn't change anything. I was the same performer and the same mover. I had the same body and the same hair. I was the same person. It's just that the songs weren't mine. And isn't that what made the biggest difference? It wasn't the look. It's interesting and ironic how it all comes together. In the end, you wind up being successful if your songs work."

If someone wants to look to her future, she said, then pay attention to her songs. The signs will be there, she says.

"The music will dictate everything," she said. "That's the way it's always been in my career. The music leads. It tells me what I should do."

For now, she can be guaranteed one thing: People will be listening. Shania's proven she can sell records; she's proven she can sell concert tickets and entertain crowds. That leaves one last thing: In a fickle world, can she prove that she can last?